Managed Services Operations Manual

Standard Operating Procedures for Computer Consultants and Managed Service Providers

Volume One: Front Office Mastery

SOPs for Office Management, Finances, Administration, and Running Your Company More Efficiently

Karl W. Palachuk

Published by

Great Little Book Publishing

Sacramento, CA

www.GreatLittleBook.com

Great Little Book Publishing
Sacramento, CA

Managed Services Operations Manual: Standard Operating Procedures for Computer Consultants and Managed Service Providers
Volume One: Front Office Mastery - SOPs for Office Management, Finances, Administration, and Running Your Company More Efficiently

Parts of this book are derived from blog posts written by Karl W. Palachuk at http://blog.smallbizthoughts.com.

ISBN 978-0-9905923-2-7 (for this volume)

ISBN 978-1-942115-03-8 (for this volume on Kindle)

ISBN 978-0-9905923-9-6 (for this volume on Smashwords)

ISBN 978-0-9905923-1-0 (for the 4-volume set)

ISBN 978-0-9905923-6-5 (for the Kindle 4-volume set)

ISBN 978-0-9905923-7-2 (for the Smashwords 4-volume set)

www.greatlittlebook.com

Electronic Contents

This book includes a few additional downloads what you will find very helpful. These include Word files, and a few other goodies.

If you purchased this book from SMB Books or Great Little Book, you should have received a download link when your purchase was completed.

If you lost that or purchased from Amazon or another reseller, you can register at www.SMBBooks.com.

Please have your purchase receipt ready to register. You'll need the Order ID. If your purchase somewhere other than SMBBooks.com, you'll need to forward proof of purchase to us.

Please respect our copyright and do not make unauthorized copies of these documents.

We welcome your feedback. Please email *karlp@greatlittlebook.com.*

Warning about Used Books

When you register your book online, you agree that the book is no longer returnable for a refund. We simply have to assume that anyone who registers the book is going to download the electronic content and use it. Therefore, the book cannot be returned once the e-version has been downloaded. That also means that the owner of a used copy of the book does not have access to the electronic content. Thank you for your support and understanding.

Managed Services Operations Manual

Standard Operating Procedures for Computer Consultants and Managed Service Providers

Volume One: Front Office Mastery

SOPs for Office Management, Finances, Administration, and Running Your Company More Efficiently

Karl W. Palachuk

Table of Contents

About The Author

Karl W. Palachuk has been an IT Consultant since 1995 and is one of the pioneers of the managed services business model. One of his books - *Managed Services in a Month* - has been the number one book on managed services on Amazon.com for more than five years.

Karl is a popular blogger among managed service providers and produces a wide variety of educational events each year, ranging from online classes, in-personal seminars, and the only all-online three-day conference in the SMB channel.

"Everything we do," says Karl, "is intended to help technology consultants be better with the business side of their business."

You can always catch up with him at www.SmallBizThoughts.com.

www.facebook.com/karlpalachuk

www.twitter.com/karlpalachuk

www.linkedin.com/in/karlpalachuk

www.pinterest.com/karlpalachuk

YouTube.com/SmallBizThoughts

www.tumblr.com/blog/smallbizthoughts

Acknowledgements

I have written or co-written eleven books before this. With this four-volume set I am publishing my 12th, 13th, 14th, and 15th books. More than any project I've ever been involved in, this set of books has been a HUGE effort and a HUGE collaborative effort.

I have over 100 people to thank for making these books possible. Some are co-workers. Some are friends. Some are business associates. And I am proud to say that some are "strangers." (Not really strangers any more since they helped with this project.)

The Story

The story of this four-volume set has three major chapters. First, I started blogging about SOPs – Standard Operating Procedures – on Fridays. I called it *SOP Friday* and even registered the domain name *SOPFriday.com*. You can still go there to get a list of blog posts in an "index" format.

Second, I put together a big fund-raising campaign at Indiegogo.com to raise money to speed up the publication process. It takes a lot of money to produce a book set like this. As a result, raising money allowed me to speed up how quickly I was able to have the money needed for design, layout, etc.

Third, I gathered up all the SOPs from the blog, plus a number that we've used in the businesses I've run over the last twenty years. I had to reorganize the contents quite a bit to make it make sense. Then I had to fill in some gaps. I was surprised at how much writing still remained. So I got to work at that.

Thanks

Huge thanks go out to my friend Monica Caraway for helping with this project. Monica serves as my Marketing Manager and spearheaded the successful Indiegogo campaign.

And of course I thank every single person who contributed to the Indiegogo campaign. Here are those who agreed to have their names published:

Lars Andersson
David Armstrong
Daniel Ashurst
Derik T Bahl
Steven Banks
Matt Beardon
Scott Bechtold
Don Bentz
Sam Berar
Frank Boecherer
Jeff Bolden
Chris Braham
Frank Bravata
Rory Breen
Sharon Broughton
Rayanne Buchianico
Lauren Buchland
Dan Buhler
MIchael Campbell
Steve Carter
Brett Chalmers
Stephanie Chandler
Jeremy Christensen
Robin Cole
Robert C Coop
Robert Coppedge
Ross Coutts
Charles Dalton
Deal Consulting, Inc.
Ana Diaz
Ryan Dobb
Benjamin Duncan
Jonathan Elliott
Raul Espino
Bob Farkas
James Forbis
Randall Garner
David P Grinder
Thomas H Lem Jr
Alan Helbush
Jonathan Henderson
Shane Hicks

Anthony Iaccino
Jamie Jensen
Maggie Jones
Leonard Keao
Jakub Kosiec
Thomas Kragh
David Libby
Joshua D Liberman
Eric Long
Steve Marfisi
Darryl McAllister
Tom McKay
Stanley Ng Kian Meng
Bob Milliken
Simon Morley
Juan Nieves
David Okeefe
Rajendra J Patel
Sheldon Penner
Scott Phillips
Dr Gary Porter
Craig Ray
Adam Rowley
Kenneth Shafter
Dewayne Smith
Vikis Sood
Gjeret Stein
Russ Swall
Thomas Tassi
Don Tibbits
John Vighetto
Mark Ward

Raffi Jamgotchian
Candice Jones
Thomas Karakis
Henry Knoop
Louie Kouvelas
Hank Leander

Michael Lindsay
Nick Mancuso
James Martin
Kenneth McDermott
Shane McParland
Bob Michie
Scott Minke
Robert Nelson
Vijay Nyayapati
Manny Oliva
Sheldon Penner
Eric Penney
Duleep Pillai
Marlon N. Ramanan
Alexander Romp
Shawn Scott
Biren Shukla
Ray Smith
Clive Start
Nathan Stone
Rich Szymanski
Sean Thompson
Kevin Tobey
Kevin Vinitsky
Josh Weiss

Michael R West	Julian Wilkinson
John Zanazzi	Ron Zayac

. . . And Thank You to the entire SMB consulting community for your continued support over all these years.

- karlp

Karl W. Palachuk

A Note About KPEnterprises

For sixteen years I owned and operated KPEnterprises Business Consulting, which has been the model for my experiences and writing over the last decade. But people and businesses evolve.

KPEnterprises was closed down at the end of 2011 and is now simply a brand name underneath Great Little Book Publishing Co., Inc. I am spending most of my time writing, consulting, and training on the "GLB" business. The old MSP business is now owned by someone else.

I do operate a small MSP with just a few clients, called Karl Palachuk Enterprises. I do that to keep my nose in the business. It keeps me up to date on strategic planning, sales, project management, and some network migrations.

I am also a business coach. I keep five or fewer clients so that I can have time to spend on writing, blogging, traveling, etc. This mix works great for me. I get to play with new technology. I get to interact with clients. I get to keep my fingers in the support side of the business.

So . . . when I refer to KPEnterprises in this book, I am either referring to the company I owned for sixteen years or the current company I work with. They are run essentially the same.

Section I

Getting Started

1

Introduction to SOPs for Technical Consultants and MSPs

SOP stands for *Standard Operating Procedures.* Those are the handy little processes that you can put in place to make everything in your company work better . . . if they're followed.

All companies have SOPs, whether formally defined or not. Essentially, you have your way of doing things. If you do things consistently, that's your standard operating procedure. I'm a dyed-in-the-wool fan of Michael Gerber's *E-Myth Revisited.* It is a great discussion about standard procedures and why they are extremely helpful for even very small businesses.

In large companies, checklists and SOPs are everywhere. In some businesses, they simply make everything consistent, productive, and profitable. In some organizations, they are absolutely critical - even life and death. Two great examples are medical surgeries and airline travel. One mistake or skipped step could be deadly.

Thankfully, most MSP jobs are a lot less critical in nature. Some people argue that you should not put standard processes in place until you're successful, have a few employees, and are ready to really grow. I think that is very short-sighted and has cost many companies a lot of money.

If you want to see the power of SOPs, examine a successful franchise. Subway sandwiches is the most popular food franchise in the world. They have a pre-defined formula for mixing the cleaner to mop the floor. In fact, it is sold by the franchise to the store in pre-measured packets along with buckets marked precisely.

UPS stores, Courtyard by Marriott, and Curves for Women all have similar policies. In a franchise, the owner is investing in a business that has already proven to work. The new owner is handed a big folder of SOPs. Unless you belong to a franchise, you need to build your own SOPs. Even with a franchise, there are plenty of details you need to formalize for yourself.

Time spent on SOPs is time spent working ON the business.

Time spent executing SOPs and delivering service is time spent working IN the business.

You need both.

There's an old saw that you should act like the person (business) you want to become. If you have sloppy procedures or do every job differently, then you won't be able to suddenly create and propagate SOP's when you start to grow. Just like any other muscles, your muscles of success will be trained to be non-standardized. You need to exercise those standardization muscles now, not when you have 50 employees.

SOPs can play at least three critical roles as you grow your company - whether you're growing the top line revenue, the bottom line profit, or both. First, SOPs can make you more profitable today. They reduce rework and bring consistency. Second, SOPs can help you grow into the company you want to be. For example, they make hiring and training new people much more efficient.

Third, having SOPs in place when you get where you're going can give you a certain "buffer" of stability. That is, while you're focused on growing the company larger, SOPs will help to minimize the effects of non-stop change upon your daily operations (and profitability). Successful processes will make you successful.

For technology businesses in general, checklists are a good fit. We do many procedures over and over. At the same time, almost all of these procedures can be done differently each time. In particular, the order in which you execute tasks can vary dramatically. Sometimes this doesn't matter, but sometimes it definitely does.

You don't have to install the servers or configure firewalls exactly like the next company, but you should consistently do these things the same way within your own company. Creating a process, a procedure, and a checklist will accomplish this. When you hire another consultant to help with a job, or hire an employee, you will be confident that the job was done "your" way.

Even if you intend to always be a sole proprietor, there are many tasks that you only execute from time to time. You need to do these consistently as well. Processes, checklists, and procedures will accomplish this.

What are Processes, Procedures, and Checklists?

We use these terms all the time, but we may not necessarily agree on their precise meaning. So here are the definitions we'll be using. When we use these terms we move from the general to the specific. So "process" describes something generally, "procedure" describes something more specifically, and "checklist" describes the finest detail.

A Process is the name given to a series of tasks that result in a general outcome. For example, you will have a process for building a server and a process for changing Internet service providers. When we use the term process, we are speaking in very general terms.

A Procedure is the name given to a specific set of action steps that achieve an outcome. A process might include several different procedures. So within the process of changing ISPs, we might have procedures for managing DNS, moving email, and reconfiguring the router. Note that some ISP moves may not include changes to email. Therefore, the general process of changing ISPs may involve different procedures at different clients.

A Checklist is the name given to the finest level of detail for executing the action steps needed to achieve a result. A procedure should include at least one checklist, but might include more than one checklist. Alternatively, a procedure might be executed with more than one checklist. For example, a "Firewall Configuration Procedure" would call out one checklist for Cisco firewalls and a different checklist for Watchguard firewalls. Even within one of these, there are different checklists for clients who need port forwarding and those who do not.

At some level, we can be a little sloppy and use these terms interchangeably. But there really is a difference. I try to use them precisely, but sometimes it just makes sense to say "processes and procedures" to refer to the whole lot.

What's the Different Between Policies and Procedures?

Policies are general rules. Procedures are steps taken to implement those rules.

Policies should be general so they are flexible and scalable, and do not have to change whenever products or technologies are adopted or retired. For example, your organization needs a policy requiring that systems must be protected against viruses and malware. That is all that the policy should say.

You should also have written procedures identifying the tool(s) you will use and your configuration requirements to comply with the policy. If you change products, you can change your procedures without going through the organizational process to modify policies. As new technologies like tablets and smart phones (and who know what will be next?) are adopted, you will not have to change policies as long as you did not address specific technologies.

How Many SOPs Do You Need?

You might be surprised to hear me say this, but you don't need SOPs for every single thing you do. Maybe someday you will. But the best practice is to create and implement them as you need them - or when you realize that you will need them.

A great example of this is the whole set of processes and procedures around hiring employees. If you create them years in advance, you're really just going through a theoretical exercise. If you create them after you hire your first employee, then you will waste a significant amount of time (and maybe money). Ideally, you will create them within a few months of your first hire.

This will be easier because it will be "real" at the time and fit your actual operation rather some future operation you can only guess at. And don't forget to update the process immediately after the hire. That way you can include all the little thing you hadn't thought of, things that need to be done in a different order, etc.

As you look through SOP worksheets, consider very seriously whether you need SOPs for every item list. (Of course you don't!)

Simply cross out the items you do not need. You might need them someday, but it's okay if you don't need them today.

As always, you need to do what's best for your business and what fits best with your business plan.

Using This Book

This book – and each book in the 4-volume set – is filled with advice. So much advice that it may be hard to figure out where to start. Do not let yourself become overwhelmed!

At the end of each chapter you'll see this graphic:

It will be accompanied by a few key points from the chapter and some places for you to make notes about changes you will implement. See the next page.

I encourage you to take notes. Put something in these pages. But also keep a notebook. Write down all your ideas. Put them in your ticketed system or goal tracking system.

Turn those ideas into actions – that's where change will take place in your business.

And if you get stuck, feel free to email me. You never know when a different perspective can help.

Three Take-Aways from This Chapter:

1. SOPs will make your business more successful in many ways.
2. A process contains one or more procedures. A procedure contains one or more checklists.
3. The best time to develop SOPs is shortly before you need them.

Three Action Steps for Your Company:

1. ____

   ____

2. ____

   ____

3. ____

   ____

2

Setting Up an MSP Office

One of the biggest decisions you need to make in the early days of your business is whether – and when – to move into an office space outside your home. If you grow and have employees, this will happen eventually. But when you're very small you can save a lot of money with a home office.

The big question here is when to move from home office to "real" office.

There are a few stages to getting set up. If you start out as a one-person shop, then starting at home makes perfect sense. Even now, after 18 years, our business could be run almost completely from our various homes. But we've had an office for ten years because we need a place to build our company culture.

Think about this: Why do you need an office?

And why do you need an office away from home?

You Need An Office To Be Efficient

You need a place where you can get your work done. It should be free from distractions. It should have a place to store company paperwork, client information, and the general "stuff" that any business accumulates.

Your office should be a well-designed refuge where you can study online or with printed books.

It should not be piled high with crap - even if you're comfortable with that. You can have all the piles you want, but there should be a distraction-free zone that allows you to focus on the work at hand.

When you can no longer be efficient at home, that's a sign that an outside office is necessary.

You Need an Office to Meet Clients

While strictly true, business clients tend to want you to come to them. So unless you do trainings, you probably don't have clients coming to your office.

If you have a repair shop and clients are bringing in equipment, then you certainly need an office.

You Need an Office for Equipment Deliveries

Sometimes you get better service and even a lower price on shipping if you have a business address instead of a residential address.

But more importantly, you need a place where deliveries can show up any time and there's someone to sign for them. And that's really an argument for a mailbox address (e.g., the UPS Store) and not for an office. If you're a one person shop, you'll be running around making money and not hanging out at the office to sign for packages.

You Need an Office for Your Employees

This is true. When I started to grow, I had an employee show up at my house a few times. It was inconvenient. So we started meeting at a coffee shop. Less convenient.

Then I wanted to hire an assistant. Turns out temp agencies don't want to send people to home offices. I understand that.

An office gives employees a place to go. They get to set up shop - even if it's a box on the shelf or a drawer to call their own. When you have an employee, that's probably the time to start looking for an office. When you have two, then you definitely need an office.

Note: You will probably start with part-time employees. You still need the office. But don't drop that mailbox address because your part time employees will not always be around to sign for packages.

Having employees come together in a common place makes it easier to have meetings, trainings, etc. It gives you a place to build machines, stage deployments, and generally play with technology.

Then There's the Downside

An office costs money. And unless you rent space in a furnished executive office building, it can cost a lot of money. You need desks, chairs, and a filing cabinet. Someone will want coffee and it won't be long before you decide you need a microwave and refrigerator.

If people have desks, they need computers and monitors. You need a white board, a network printer, paper, pens, staplers, tape, and all the other joyous things that go in offices.

You also need insurance.

We love the insurance program through The ASCII Group (www.ascii.com) has a great insurance program for liability, property, and even worker's comp.

When you have employees you need worker's compensation insurance. This can be very expensive. You also have various other expenses that I just lump into the category of "taxes." These include Social Security (you pay 6.2% of the employee's salary into this) along with Medicare, state unemployment, federal unemployment, etc.

In all, plan on spending 10-15% above the hourly rate for employee expenses. If you offer medical or other benefits, then it's more.

There Are Long Term Benefits

As I mentioned, we could probably work with no office whatsoever. America's Tech Support (my former MSP) and Great Little Book shared the same office for ten year. If we all just went home and stayed there, we would lose quite a bit of what our companies have become.

In addition to the culture, having an office infrastructure in place makes it a lot easier to grow and shrink as needed. If you need to hire some folks, you've got a place to put them. You can get interns and have a place for them to show up.

With an office you have lots of great flexibility to work and play together. Again, building culture is much easier with a common meeting place.

Overall, my advice would be this:

- If you're a sole proprietor, put off getting an office as long as possible (assuming you can work efficiently at home). This will save you a LOT of money.

- When you start to have employees, start looking for an office. If you believe you're going to grow and have an employee for the foreseeable future, get an office.
- Buy things only when you need them.
- Create a realistic budget of what it will cost to have a "real" office outside the home.

Looking around my office now I realize that all the furniture and equipment is pretty nice and pretty new. When we started it was a collection of yard sale stuff that was good enough to get by. Over time we traded up and up as we needed more desks, chairs, etc.

At this point I think I might always have an office just because it's so convenient for many things.

Three Take-Aways from This Chapter:

1. Avoid the expense of an office as long as you can.
2. Determine the point at which you will get an office so you can start planning.
3. When the time comes, make a budget.

Three Action Steps for Your Company:

1. ______________________________

   ____

2. ______________________________

   ____

3. ______________________________

   ____

3

Getting Started: Naming Your Business

Picking a good business name is an important part of starting your business. And, under certain circumstances, you might even rename your business. Here are some thoughts for picking a successful name.

Choosing a Name Based on The Formation of Your Company

Your company might be a sole proprietorship (doing business under your own Social Security Number/Tax ID). Or you might be a corporation (S corp or C corp), or an LLC, or a variety of other entities. This only matters for a few things.

First, you cannot use a title such as "Inc." when you are a sole proprietor. In some states it is illegal. But it's always misleading. Legally, when you sign contracts, you need to sign them with your name and title. This might be ...

John Doe, d.b.a. My I.T. Company

Jane Doe, President, My I.T. Company

John Doe, President, My I.T. Company, Inc.

It's important that, whatever the name of your company, you sign documents correctly. If you are not a sole proprietor, signing documents incorrectly could make you personally liable rather than your company - exactly what you want to avoid.

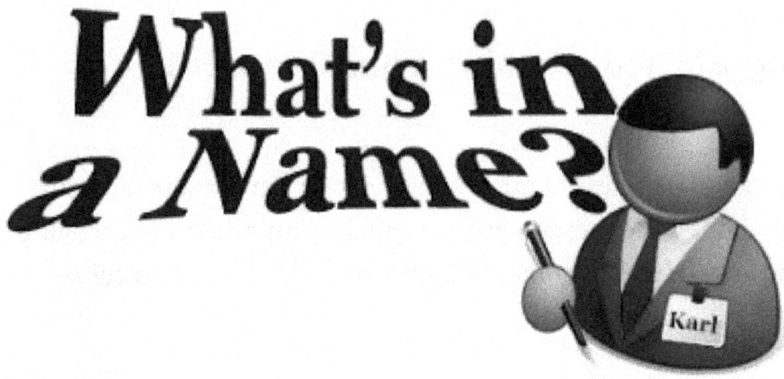

Second, if you move from a Sole Proprietor (Sole Trader in the UK) to a corporation or other form of business, you may want to take the opportunity to change your name. You don't have to, but you'd be surprised at what a difference it can make.

My business was originally KPEnterprises just because I'm KP and I don't have a huge imagination. When I incorporated, I changed the name to KPEnterprises Business Consulting, Inc. This sounded a little more formal and stuffy. And guess what? One of my long-standing clients called me and said, "I see you're doing business consulting now. Can you come by and help us with a problem?"

Of course I said yes. The cool thing is that even people who knew me took a different view of my business once the name changed.

Choose a Professional Business Name

Pick a good, professional name for your business. If you want to charge top rates, be taken seriously, and make it easy for people to give you referrals, then you need a good name.

As a general rule, you should avoid cute and gimmicky names. Instead, tend toward professional business-like names. As I've said before, I don't want to hire the Lawyer Wizards to represent my company. I don't want the Plumbing Guru to magically fix my pipes.

In Sacramento we have a transmission repair shop that used to be called the Transmission Nerds. Maybe it's just me, but I don't put a lot of faith in a company with a name like that. If we want to be professionals, we need to be aware of the kinds of companies that have respect among our clients.

If you're just forming a business, or reformulating your business, try to pick a name that sounds business-like. Ideally, your business name should state what you do. Computers, mobile, networks, and business consulting are fine. Partner names are great (e.g., Johnson and Andrews), as are local landmarks (tower, lake, Sierra, valley, etc.).

Here are some more good names:

_____ Associates

_____ and Co.

_____ Professionals

_____ Resources

_____ Technical Resources

I have high hopes that our field will become more professional over time. Perhaps a byproduct of that will be the gradual disappearance of gurus, geeks, and cyber-goobers.

Just my opinion.

Changing Your Business Names

If you want a more professional name, incorporate, or just want to rebrand, don't worry about your existing client base. You might resist getting rid of a cutesy name because your ego gets in the way. If so, you have to decide how much your ego is worth.

One of the guys in the Sacramento SMB I.T. Pro group has changed his business name three times in the last twenty years. Note that he's still in business after twenty years! He never lost a client because he changed the business name.

In my own case, the move from KPEnterprises to KPEnterprises Business Consulting, Inc. was very minor and few existing customers really noticed. Later, when Mike took over the business, he adopted the name America's Tech Support, which is a sole proprietorship. We sent letters to our clients and asked them to change the name in their accounts.

No one mentioned it or questioned it. To existing clients, the name change was an extremely minor event.

New prospects didn't know, of course. The new name sounds nice and has no negative connotations. We do lose a bit of brand awareness, since KPEnterprises had operated and advertised that name for sixteen years. But this was a minor issue.

Ideally, any name change will be a long-term change. So take it seriously. Think of it as an opportunity to start your branding from scratch. In fact, that's exactly what it is.

Which Comes First: Company Name or Domain Name?

On several occasions I've mentioned to groups of consultants that I have several Internet domain names registered. Basically, whenever an idea pops into my head, I try to register several domain names for it. I have about 300 domains in total.

Sometimes the domain names I register are the name of a product, service, or company. Other times, they are additional "landing page" domains so I can use Google, Facebook, Twitter, LinkedIn, and blogs to funnel traffic to my primary sites.

But of course you will have one primary domain name. It should be as simple and easy to remember as possible. Many of the techno-goobery names discussed above are very difficult to convey to people by phone. Again, cutesy doesn't work well.

One of the important considerations these days is whether your domain name "matches" your company name. And then, do you name the domain after the company or name the company after the domain? I don't know if there's a right answer here.

Many very professional companies have domain names that are not their company name. Go down your list of clients and you'll see this, especially with service professions such as attorneys, doctors, and accountants. But you should try to get your company name and domain name as close as possible.

The good news on the domain name front is that people are now used to long domain names. It used to be that three- and four-letter domains were hot because they are short. But that's less of an issue today. So a name like Americas Tech Support can get away with americastechsupport.com.

Let me jump back to the discussion of choosing a professional name for a moment. If you have a company name and a domain name that are descriptive of what you do, this can help with some very basic search engine optimization. After all, if someone searches for

"Alhambra Computer Services" and your company name is Alhambra Computer Services, and your domain is alhambracomputerservices.com, you should be right up at the top of the results.

You're probably happy with your business name, and don't plan on starting a new division anytime soon. But if do need to adopt a new business name, I hope these thoughts are helpful.

Three Take-Aways from This Chapter:

1. Avoid cutesy business names
2. Try to get a domain name that matches your business.
3. Naming your business is the most fundamental branding.

Three Action Steps for Your Company:

1. ____

____

2. ____

____

3. ____

____

4

Getting Started: The Form of Your Business

When you start out, you need to decide on the form of your business. That means, what will your business be legally and for tax purposes?

The first step in defining your relationship with your client is to define who you are. Are you a sole proprietor? Are you a corporation? An LLC? Something else?

There are really only a few ways to define yourself. And, really, the two default methods are sole proprietor and S-Corp. We'll discuss why below. Pretty much everyone starts out as a sole proprietor. Once you get to a certain size, or a certain salary, then S-Corp makes sense.

To your clients, only two things matter:

- "To whom do I make the check?"

and

- "Do I need to send 1099s at the end of the year?"

Other than that, the only time you really need to pay attention to how your business is legally defined is in your service agreements. Of particular importance is the question of getting out of the way of the Tax Man.

Forming Your Consultancy

I'm sure you're a very nice person. But if I were to engage in business with you, I'd want to make sure that your personal "stuff" doesn't get all mixed up with my personal "stuff." If you've ever been a landlord, you know what I mean. In business, we need to separate our personal financial life from our professional financial life.

In general, I think that sole proprietors should re-address the question of incorporation every few years. In particular, if you are successful, then revisiting the benefits is in order.

Another area affected by your business form is your status as an employer. When you hire people, then you have a whole new world of taxes and forms and filings. And now you have your personal stuff exposed to your employees' personal stuff.

Important Safety Tip: Don't Mess With the IRS

People go bankrupt when they ignore the IRS's instructions. This is not for you.

You need to be very careful to make sure that your service agreements are written so that you cannot be considered an employee of your clients. You can say "I'm not."

But that only goes so far. The IRS rules change all the time, but two issues will always affect independent consultants. First, the question of whether the client should be withholding taxes from your "paycheck." Second, the question of whether you can take a home office deduction. On both questions I'm deep into the "play it safe" school of thought.

We're not going to look at the home office deduction very closely as it's not the focus of this post. But you need to talk to your CPA or

Enrolled Agent and take his advice. As for the tax man, go to http://www.irs.gov and do a search of "home office."

On the question of employee versus independent contractor, there are several items you should have in your service agreements that define this relationship. Again, to find out the latest rules and regulations, go to http:// www.irs.gov and search for "Employee or Independent Contractor?" You might also look at IRS form SS-8, "Determination of Worker Status for Purposes of Federal Employment Taxes and Income Tax Withholding."

Just so you know, the tax man doesn't care how you see yourself or your relationship with the client. The tax man has some very specific ideas about whether or not you're an employee. The general rule is: If the client controls what will be done and how it will be done, then the client is your employer.

Of course this is broken down into specific discussions. For example, if the client tells you where to be, when to be there, how to get the job done, what tools to use, who to hire, where to buy supplies, and in what sequence work must be performed, then you are an employee.

Similarly, if the client pays for training, you might be an employee.

You might look at the IRS publications and find yourself on a borderline for one or more regulations. That's where contracts or service agreements come in. The IRS specifically states that one of the criteria for defining the relationship is to specify that relationship in a contract.

So, you see why it's important to make sure you never do any work without some kind of agreement. Even a basic "Credit Agreement" should cover the basics of the relationship. If anyone balks at signing this, you can tell them two things. First, you won't work without it. And, second, one of the goals is to define your relationship so they don't have to withhold taxes and put you on their payroll.

As for the longer service agreements, just make sure you cover all the major points the IRS might want to look at. State very specifically that you, the consultant, will determine what needs to be done, what tools are necessary, the order in which work will be performed, etc. Also state very plainly that you are a contractor and not an employee, and that you'll pay your own taxes.

And that's the key to success – who's paying all those taxes? After all, the IRS does not exist to make the world a better place (which is good, because they suck at it). The IRS exists to collect various kinds of taxes. You don't have to specify that you'll pay your Federal taxes, and your state taxes, and your unemployment taxes, etc. But it goes a long ways to have a signed agreement that both you and the client know that you are paying your taxes.

If you are the kind of consultant who actually "goes to work" at a client's office, has a desk to sit at, and you perform most or all of your work there, you need to be particularly careful about these regulations. You also need to be extremely careful about taking a home office deduction.

The bottom line: Find out what the current rules are and rely on professionals for advice. The tax business is just as fast-paced as the computer business. By the time something gets printed, it's probably out of date. Find a good Certified Public Accountant or Enrolled Agent to advise you on these matters. And make sure you have a lawyer review your service agreements!

If you need a good book on contracts, I would be honored if you would take a look at *Service Agreements for SMB Consultants*, a book I wrote specifically for this industry. It goes into this topic in great detail and includes sample language.

Define Yourself: Sole Proprietor

Perhaps the “default configuration” for an independent contractor is to be a sole proprietor. That means that you are just you for tax purposes. Part of you runs a business, and that part of you has to fill out Schedule C on your income taxes.

Legally it means that you personally are doing business with each of your clients. There is no entity between you and your clients, such as a corporation. Unless your business name is your name, then you need to file a DBA (“Doing Business As”) or Fictitious Business Name filing with some government agency. This varies state to state.

For example, my business started out as a sole proprietorship. I was Karl W. Palachuk, DBA KPEnterprises. That allowed me to get a bank account under the name KPEnterprises. But it was still associated with MY personal tax ID number. Clients could write checks to KPEnterprises or to Karl Palachuk. It didn't matter because we were one and the same.

You can grow very large and remain a sole proprietor. If you ask your clients you might find some surprisingly large companies that are really sole proprietorships.

You can have employees, buy equipment, and depreciate assets. You can do 99% of all the things any other business does.

The advantage of being a sole proprietor is that it’s easy. You just start selling services and goods. You pay your bills, you collect money. If you make a profit, that goes onto your personal tax return and you pay taxes.

If you have a professional do your taxes, it’s certainly cheaper to do one extra Schedule C than to do a corporate tax return in addition to a personal tax return. So there’s an advantage there.

The disadvantages of a sole proprietorship (in my opinion) are all financial. First, your business is your personal life. Your “stuff ” is mixed up with your clients' "stuff." In particular, if your client is also a sole proprietor, then their personal stuff is mixed with your personal stuff.

I know that bad things almost never happen. In twenty years of owning businesses (seven years as a sole proprietor), I never even had a small hint of a problem along these lines. Nobody came after my house, no one put a lien on the contents of my garage, etc. But it is a fact that a sole proprietorship is just you personally and you need to be aware of that.

You can limit your exposure to lawsuits by purchasing Errors and Omissions insurance. I believe lawsuits are rare, but you still need to take seriously the possibility that someone will sue your business.

A second disadvantage to a sole proprietorship is the self-employment tax. This falls into the category of "Don't get me started!" If you are an employee, roughly 6.5% of your wages goes to Social Security, where it is immediately loaned to the Federal Government for research on wasteful spending habits of political hacks. But you're not alone. Your employer matches this amount. So, really, a number equivalent to 13% of your income is flushed down the government toilet.

When you are self-employed (as a sole proprietor is), you get to pay both sides of this, which is fine. If you were a corporation, you would also pay both sides, but you the person and you the corporation would each pay 6.5%. But here's the bad news:

As a sole proprietor, all of your profit is considered your personal income. If you earn $60,000, you pay Social Security taxes on $60,000. If you make $90,000, you pay Social Security on all $90,000.

If you were an S-Corp, you'd pay yourself a salary and pay the Social Security only on your salary. The rest of the profit from the business would flow to you as "dividends." So, let's say you pay yourself that very reasonable $60,000 salary. You pay the Social Security on $60,000.

But you don't pay the Social Security on the remaining $30,000. Thirteen percent of $30,000 is $3,900! That's a chunk of change. You'd still pay your regular tax rate on that $30,000, but not the Social Security. Note that you don't pay Social Security taxes after a certain income level (currently around $114,000, but this goes up every year). Your numbers may be very different.

For more information on Social Security taxes, see http://www.ssa.gov/policy/docs/quickfacts/prog_highlights.

The point is simple, however. There's a lot of money at stake here and you should give some serious consideration to how your company is formed. Note that you cannot pay yourself a miserably low salary to avoid Social Security taxes. The basic rule for the IRS is pretty simple. If you do something just to avoid taxes, it's not allowed. So you can't pay yourself minimum wage and take $50,000 in dividends.

Again, don't mess with the IRS.

But also remember that you are allowed to take normal, reasonable, legal actions to reduce your taxes. Creating a corporation for your business is certainly a normal business activity.

I am not a tax professional. Don't do something just because I presented some ideas here. Find a qualified tax professional and go over the numbers. If you're in that $60,000-$115,000 range, you might save yourself some money.

At a minimum, don't dismiss the idea because it seems complicated or tax prep will become more expensive. A good tax pro will always save you money.

Define Yourself: S-Corp

When you decide to incorporate your business, you automatically form a Subchapter C Corporation or C-Corp. You must then file Federal form 2553 in order to "elect" to become a Subchapter S Corporation or S-Corp.

The primary difference between the two, for small entities, is that C-Corps pay taxes on the corporation's profits and stockholders also pay taxes on any dividend disbursements. With an S-Corp, the corporation does not pay taxes. It files a tax form to determine what the profit is, then that profit flows to the income calculation on the stockholders' personal income tax form.

In other words, with a C-Corp your income is taxed twice. There are other advantages for C-Corps that make sense for large entities. But for closely held companies (e.g., you, or you and a spouse, or you and one other person) the S-Corp is really the only option to consider.

The key benefit of a corporation is that you can avoid paying the Social Security or Self Employment Tax on a portion of your income. See the discussion of Sole Proprietorships, above. There are also several deductions available as a corporation that are not available as a Sole Proprietor.

Another major benefit of the Corporation form of business is that the business is an entity unto itself. In fact, legally it is a person, which is bizarre. With a corporation, you personally have a relationship with the corporation and the corporation has a relationship with your clients. So you have this layer that protects your stuff from their stuff.

With a corporation, you have a certain level of liability protection. If someone sues the business, they can't normally get to your personal possessions. I say "normally" because you have to take certain actions to maintain this "corporate veil." If you treat the corporation like your personal ATM and don't treat it like a corporation, the courts are likely to say that you did not maintain it as a corporation. So that puts your possessions back out there for lawsuits.

Corporations don't make sense when you're first starting out unless you got some great long-term, highly profitable contracts. Generally speaking, you need to maintain a certain level of profitability – and expect that to continue – before you incorporate.

Note also that corporate tax rates vary from state to state. There may be minimum taxes due, even in a year when the corporation loses money.

If you are considering a corporation, find a tax pro who deals with corporations. Agree to pay an hourly fee and sit down with your financial information and "run the numbers." Get a best-guess estimate of what you'd pay in taxes as a corporation versus a sole proprietor.

Finding a great tax professional is extremely important. And we tend to become personally attached to these folks. But your primary concern needs to be your business.

And it may be the case that you need to find "the next level" of skill and ability in a tax professional so that your business can move to the next level.

One final note on corporations. If you grow and are successful, you will eventually form a corporation. If you always stay just one person, you may choose not to incorporate.

But if you hire people and start growing, there are too many advantages to not incorporate.

Define Yourself: LLC, Partnerships, etc.

Once you move away from Sole Proprietorship and S-Corp, there's whole alphabet soup of options available, including:

- General Partnership
- Limited Partnership
- Limited Liability Partnership
- Limited Liability Company
- and additional entities available in individual states.

Partnerships are generally to be avoided. They are easy to set up, but they provide no protection of your personal stuff from your own business partner. So, if things go bad, they can go very bad. If you invest in real estate, revisit this issue for that enterprise, but not for your technical consulting business.

LLCs aren't bad. They act a lot like corporations, but allow profits to be allocated by means other than percent of business owned. They tend to be more expensive to create than a corporation, and state laws governing LLCs can be different from Federal laws.

Again, I sound like a broken record here, but you need to do your research and check with your tax and legal advisers.

Generally, you should have a solid business reason for choosing the form of your business. And for almost everyone, that choice will come down to being either a sole proprietor or an S-Corp. If someone suggests that you create some other entity, make sure you understand why.

It never hurts to get a second opinion.

Concluding Thoughts

How you define your form of business will have little direct effect on how you write your Service Agreements or operate your business. Remember to play your role at all times. If you're a sole proprietor, act like a sole proprietor. If you're an S-Corp, act like an S-Corp. And so on.

Some clients will request a W-9 form, which is a statement relieving them of the responsibility of withholding taxes from your "pay." You should fill these out for anyone who asks. If you are a Sole Proprietor, you must give this information to each client. Consider filling out one form and photocopying it for each new client.

You may not really need to supply these documents to companies with whom you have a signed agreement, but just do it. They have their own bureaucracies and the person asking you for the form is just doing her job. Even as a corporation, we create a form, photocopy it, and give a copy to everyone. We also email them as PDF documents when requested.

Three Take-Aways from This Chapter:

1. Find a good accountant or tax professional. A great one if you can.
2. Consider the options and make a conscious choice about the legal form your business takes.
3. If you make $60,000 to $115,000, look into the tax savings of incorporation.

Three Action Steps for Your Company:

1. ______________________________

____

2. ______________________________

____

3. ______________________________

____

5

Getting Started: Cash vs. Accrual Accounting

One of the big(ish) decisions you need to make about your business is whether you will use the Cash Method or the Accrual Method of accounting. You can switch from one to the other, but it's not a good idea to do that too frequently. At the rollover to a new year is a good time to switch if you decide to.

What Are Cash Accounting and Accrual Accounting?

These are the two options you have for keeping track of money coming into and going out of your business. The essential difference between these two methods is the timing of when you "earn" or "spend" money. With cash basis, you earn money on the day you receive it and you spend money on the day you pay it. With accrual basis, you earn money on the day you invoice the client and you spend money on the day you agree to pay for something.

Here are two examples, one for income and one for expenses.

First, let's say you invoice a client for $100 on January 2nd and she pays you on January 15th. With the cash method, you earned that money on January 15th - the day she paid. With the accrual method, you earned that money on January 2nd - the day you invoiced her.

The difference doesn't matter much - except when you're trying to keep track of how you're doing each month. If you invoice the client on January 2nd and she pays on February 2nd, that money was earned in February under the cash method. And if she doesn't pay until March, it will be earned in March. Under the accrual method, the money was earned in January no matter when the client pays.

Second, let's say you put office supplies on your credit card on January 2nd. The bill comes and you pay it on February 2nd. Under the cash method, that expense happened in February. Under the accrual method, the expense happened in January when you committed to paying for the products.

		Cash Basis	Accrual Basis
Event	**Date**	**Cash Method**	**Accrual Method**
Invoice Client	December 15th		Revenue booked Dec 15
Client Pays	December 20th	Revenue booked Dec 20	
Parts Ordered	December 27th		Expense booked Dec 27
Parts Paid For	January 15th	Expense booked Jan 15	

Table 5-1: Cash vs. Accrual Examples

Oddball Things That Happen with Cash and Accrual Methods

Personally, I think the accrual method is better for me because I like to line up income and cost of goods sold within the same month. This will never line up perfectly, but is much easier with accrual.

In my opinion, the cash method is fine if you are not good at paying attention to your financials and your bank account. But it makes it difficult to answer the simple questions:

- What were your sales last month?

and

- What were your expenses last month?

Strictly speaking, the accrual method gives you a more accurate picture of how you did each month in terms of money "earned" and money spent. But if you don't get prepaid for all your work, you need to make sure you understand that the sales represent commitments for sales, not actual dollars in your bank account. You might have $20,000 in sales but not see the money for some time to come.

The exact opposite can happen with the cash method. You might have horrible sales in December but it looks like a great month because lots of clients decide to pay their bill before the end of the year. So all that cash "income" you earned in November and October shows up in December. Then again, the slow sales in December will make January look slow even if you make lots of sales.

The only real problem with the accrual method is when the client never pays. So, for example, you booked income in January but the money never shows up. At some point you need to write off that sale so that it reduces your earnings. Otherwise, you'll be taxed on a sale even though you never got the actual money.

Which Method is Best for You?

I don't know. Go talk to your accountant.

I'm not an accountant. I pay very close attention to my numbers. I use accrual.

There are a few choices made for you by the government. If you make $5 million or more, you have to use accrual. You also have to use accrual if you have revenue over $1 million and you maintain an inventory of merchandise.

In other words, if you're small and plan to stay there, they you can choose either method. If you are a little larger then you need to use accrual.

Go talk to your accountant so that you can make a decision and understand the consequences of the decision for your business.

Three Take-Aways from This Chapter:

1. Make sure you understand the difference between cash and accrual.
2. Pick a method and stick with it.
3. Find a good accountant and take their advice. Make sure you understand it.

Three Action Steps for Your Company:

1. ____

____

2. ____

____

3. ____

____

6

Getting Started in Business: Licenses, etc.

One of the most daunting tasks when you set up your business is to make sure you have the licenses, tax identification numbers, and accounts. Luckily, most government agencies are pretty good with posting these on their web site.

But you might not know that you need to go to their web site! Here are some tips for making sure you're legal and ready for business.

Form Matters

We've already discussed Naming Your Business. The "form" of your business matters in this discussion because it will affect how you are taxed. At least in the U.S., a Sole Proprietor uses a personal Social Security Number as the Federal Tax ID.

But here's the thing. There really is no Federal Tax ID. There's an Employer ID

Number - EIN. If you are a Sole Proprietor but you have employees, you cannot pay yourself a "salary" through the payroll system. You simply keep the profits and you are responsible for making quarterly tax payments. But you pay your employees through some kind of payroll system. And for that you need a Federal EIN.

Start Here for the Federal Government:
http://www.irs.gov/Businesses/Small-Businesses-&-Self-Employed/Starting-a-Business

(Note: From time to time the IRS revises their web site and brakes most links that you'll find in a Google Search. So go to the IRS site first and then search from there.)

Normally, you can apply for an EIN online and it will be issued almost immediately. The last time I did it, it took 15 minutes to receive my EIN. Every business entity (LLC, S-Corp, etc.) must have a separate EIN if you will be paying employees.

Having said all that, when anyone asks you for your Federal Tax ID, you give them your EIN.

For most people, that's pretty much all you need from the Federal government at this point. Assuming you're in I.T. consulting, you don't need permits for transporting explosives, alcohol, or other Federally-Regulated items. So now you can move to the State government.

Reading Assignment One

Somewhere on the IRS site you'll find a link to Small Business-Related Publications. As of this writing it is at http://www.irs.gov/Businesses/Small-Businesses-&-Self-Employed/Recommended-Reading-for-Small-Businesses. Browse through that and make sure that you have some idea of the rules and requirements that apply to your business.

It should be clear right away that you need a good tax professional. Go get one if you don't have one.

State Government Requirements

Some states issue a separate state tax ID. All of them use the Federal EIN or SSN as a reference point to cross-check your Federal tax return with state tax returns and other state activities. Here the world begins to get a little complicated. Your best starting place for information is the U.S. Small Business Administration web site. It is not always up to date, but they try very hard. And you are guaranteed to miss something if you don't check out their site.

A great resource page is at http://www.sba.gov/content/learn-about-your-state-and-local-tax-obligations. It is a starting place for determining your obligations in each state. The most common kinds of taxes at the state level are:

- State Income Tax
- State Sales Tax
- Unemployment Insurance
- Workers Compensation

But there are lots of others that may apply. Start with the SBA and then find your individual state's web site. The good news is that most of the taxes and registrations you have to take care of are almost automatic when you take care of a few items.

You also have to register your business somehow. If you create a corporation or other tax entity, that will be done at the state level. So you'll get a state Tax ID as part of that process. When you file state taxes, the forms will include required payments for misc. items. When you collect and file sales tax, all the little stuff you never knew was hidden inside the sales tax code will be inside the forms you complete. When you pay employees, you'll shell out money for Federal Unemployment, State Unemployment, Social Security, and a myriad of other taxes that employees don't realize you pay.

Reading Assignment Two

Find the State web site that has all the juicy information and links related to business in your state. Every state is different. Some are very different. Again, read through all this and make links. It's up to YOU to make sure you're inside the law. State agencies have no obligation to inform you of your requirements. They just have the power to punish you if you do not comply.

Local Agencies and Licenses

There are three common types of "local" government agencies in most states. There are Counties (or Parishes) that cover a fairly large area. There are Cities (and Towns) that cover a smaller area. And then there are Special Districts that cut across city and county boundaries. For example, a utility district might supply water or electricity in an area that crosses several city and county boundaries. School districts are often within a county or within a city, but also often cross those boundaries. The same is true with fire districts. Transportation districts almost always cross city and county boundaries.

All of these districts might have taxes and regulations that apply to you.

The two easiest places to start are the county and city. One or both of these will need to issue you a business license, which is just that: A license to do business in their boundaries. You might need to get business licenses in several cities if you provide services in cities other than where your business is physically located. One of these entities will also deal with a D.B.A. if you need one. That's a "Doing Business As" statement or Fictitious Business Name application. Basically, if you have one legal I.D. such as Joe D. Plumber and you do business as Super-Good Tech Support, that you need a D.B.A.

One of these entities (city or county) is likely to have a good resource for all the local agencies and districts you need to deal with. Some will actually be able to accept forms on behalf of such agencies. Ideally, someone will point you to a golden web site that covers all the stuff you need to do to set up shop in your city/county.

Reading Assignment Three

You guessed it. Find the local web site that has all the juicy information you need to stay inside the law and make sure you are paying all the little fees and taxes that are required. Truer words have never been said than these: "The power to tax is the power to destroy." And since you are responsible for these taxes and fees whether you know it or not, it's up to you to know.

Another great resource in some locations is the local Chamber of Commerce. Sometimes, the local Chamber will have the golden web site you are looking for. Other times they'll be able to point you in the right direction.

A Google search for "Starting a business in [state]" should get you to some good starting places.

It's More Than Taxes

In addition to just paying taxes, you also have to make sure you're inside the law with all kinds of other things. You've seen the employment posters that take up the entire wall in almost every break room in America. You need those.

- You might also need to be registered with the local fire department so they can do regular inspections
- You might need a license to do work in people's homes or businesses
- You might have to register with an agency just to let them know that you are operating or paying wages within their district

And so on.

I am amazed at how many layers there are. Some states are better than others. I know California is one of the worst. But you can plow through it! Just remember that most of the businesses around you have successfully navigated these waters. (I say most, because many of them have not done this homework and will get a very big surprise one day when a government agency drops a big fine on their desk.)

Do your homework. Don't be one of the businesses that's driven out of business because you accidentally didn't file all the right paperwork or pay all the feeds.

Good luck out there.

Three Take-Aways from This Chapter:

1. Educate yourself on Federal, State, and Local business requirements.
2. Make sure you have all the Tax IDs needed at each level.
3. Ask other successful business owners for any "gotchas" regarding local taxes and laws.

Three Action Steps for Your Company:

1. ______________________________

2. ______________________________

3. ______________________________

7

How to Work 8AM to 5PM in I.T. Consulting

One of my never-ending themes is that you CAN work a normal business day. Whether that's 8AM to 5PM or 9-6, or even 8-6, "normal business day" is somewhere in that category. At least 99% of the time. So you might have three or four exceptions per year. But you can design your business to work normal hours.

This chapter addresses some thoughts about why you should work no more than about 50 hours a week and how you can work "normal" hours.

It seems like - at the small end of SMB - there has always been an assumption that you have to work after hours. Sometimes it's easier to get a job done without pesky clients around. Sometimes clients ask for it. And very often, we're simply not willing to put in the effort to figure out how to get things done while the office is in full swing.

My brother Manuel and I spent years developing a system for migrating entire networks with zero downtime. It takes a lot of planning and discovery, but it's not particularly "difficult." One of the things we tell people is that they probably already have all the skills they need. It's just a matter of having a process. (See *The Network Migration Workbook*)

Believe You Can Work 9-5

When I mention in a presentation that we don't work evenings and weekends, I always get the exact same response - after TEN YEARS of talking about this: "Well what do you do when a server crashes in the middle of the night?"

Really? That's your defense for working twelve hours a day and abandoning your family?

I'm trying to remember. I think we've had maybe two servers actually crash in the middle of the night since 1995. We are not going to build a business practice around the remote exception to the rule. If you have servers crashing left and right, you're in the wrong business.

Anyway . . . You've simply gotten in the habit of working late, answering the phone after hours, and letting clients talk you into working after hours. If you want to work evenings and weekends, that's fine. Admit that you choose to do it, and do it proudly. But don't argue that you have to or that the business requires it. You don't have to and the business does not require it.

The first step is to believe that you work normal hours. Here are a few key beliefs and behaviors that affect your beliefs about this topic:

1) Everyone does it. No. Many people in the SMB space do not work evenings and weekends. And almost no one in the mid-market or enterprise space does - Unless they are extremely well paid for it.

2) Once your clients have your cell phone, they can get your attention any time. No. You don't have to answer your phone. More on this in a minute.

3) Ignoring clients or not being available in the evening is bad customer service. No. Every business gets to set their legitimate boundaries. Being available during your normal business hours is expected. Bad customer service would be ignoring clients at that time. Almost every business you deal with is unavailable evenings and weekends.

4) Clients expect it. Yes, kind of. If you've trained them to expect it, then they expect it. Now you need to re-train them. I'll bet most of your clients have never expected you to be available during "off" hours.

Sometimes clients just use whatever communication medium is in front of them. If they're on Facebook they Facebook. If they're on email, they email. If they have an icon on their desktop that opens a ticket in your client access portal, then they open a ticket. In most cases, the client is simply trying to make sure that their issue is in your system. They don't expect an answer/fix right now. They just need to get it out of their head and into yours. They will leave a voice mail and wait. You need to provide good customer service by addressing their issue the next business day.

5) I have to. The job requires it. No. This is the 21st century. We have robust hardware and software. We have remote monitoring and access tools. We have help desk support that's paid to be awake when we're asleep. We have techniques and processes that it possible to do virtually everything during business hours.

Here's an interesting question: How many of your client are available 24x7 to THEIR clients with no minimums and no after-hour rates. I'm just going to speculate here, but I'll bet that number is zero for almost everyone reading this.

Every consulting company that grows big has some rules about overtime. They're not the same for everyone, but here are some of the basics.

- Employees work 40-hour weeks
- Employees get paid for overtime
- Client work is done during normal business hours (8am-5pm)
- Clients pay extra for work outside those hours

As strange as it sounds, it can be very profitable to move into these policies. So, if you're not doing them, start soon. It is quite reasonable that, on a 30-day notice, you can raise your after-hours rates. That will make you more money and reduce the number of after-hours hours.

It is highly unlikely that you will ever grow your business beyond a one- or two-person shop until you adopt the policies you need to sustain a larger company.

Balancing Your Work and Life

Some people are born to be state workers. They naturally clock in at 8:00 AM and clock out at 5:00 PM and never think about work any other time. But most of the human race ENJOYS working. It gives us pleasure. It makes us feel useful and valuable.

It's very common to talk to IT Pros that really love their clients and see their job as a service they are performing. There are people who make life bad for others and there are people who make life better for others. Service providers (including IT service providers) provide a service that truly helps people. We make their businesses more efficient. We save them money. We help them to do things they couldn't do before.

The point is simple: It's okay to love your work. In fact, it's one of the greatest feelings in the world. When your business is "in the zone" you can get a lot of pleasure from it. So it's good to love work.

But you can't just work. You need to have a balanced life. You need to have hobbies. You need to blow off steam. You need to find great pleasure in other things.

As a writer, I always have several projects going at once. I try to lay them out on tables so they are visible to me and easily accessible. The reason is simple: Sometimes I have energy for one project and not another. I will work on the project that I get the most enjoyment out of. But sometimes I have a deadline and have to work on a specific project whether I like it or not. Even then, I can switch to another project for a short while and balance out my day.

Sometimes your job gives you energy and sometimes it takes your energy. This changes all the time. That's one reason why you need to find happiness and energy in the other parts of your life: Your personal life, you family life, your hobbies, your sports, etc. Giving each of these some of your attention will make you happier and more energetic overall.

"The balance" is different for everyone, so I can't say that you should do what I do. But I CAN say that working 16 hours a day is bad for your health, bad for your business, and bad for your personal life. If you're working those kind of hours, things are very un-balanced.

You have to work at balance. It won't happen by itself.

Making the Change to Working Normal Hours

So, how do you re-formulate your company so that you really work normal hours and your clients understand that? Here are some tips.

First, decide you will do this. There may be a transition period, but it will be harder on you than on your clients. You have a habit all the time. Each client only needs after-hours assistance once in awhile. You have to figure out what you're going to do when you're not working.

Second, adopt the simple policies mentioned above:

- Employees work 40-hour weeks - Including YOU
- Employees get paid for overtime
- Client work is done during normal business hours (8am-5pm) Monday-Friday
- Clients pay extra for work outside those hours

Third, if you need to amend contracts, do so. The most common rates for after-hours work are time-and-a-half (1.5x) and double-time (2x). Pick one and use it. You may want to give a 30 day notice to clients without a contract. Better yet, use this as an excuse to sign a contract with all your clients.

Fourth, set a transition period for yourself. Maybe three months. During that period, don't answer your phone after hours, but return calls if you think it's important. But wait longer and longer to return calls.

If a client asks you to do work, simply say, "I want to make sure you know the after-hours rate is $300/hr. So you can save a lot of money if this can wait."

Clients will almost always wait. They only asked you to work after hours because it cost them nothing extra. Now that there's a cost, you will see a quick change in behavior.

Fifth, be prepared for zero backlash. In reality, this will affect very few clients. And they will understand and come into line quickly. After all, these are very reasonable policies.

If you get in the habit of working too much, it feeds on itself and you feel that you can't get out: you can't change the way things are.

That's not true. Just decide to change. You can make it happen.

Three Take-Aways from This Chapter:

1. Commit to working normal hours. Set a timeline for implementing this.
2. Set your after-hours rates and let clients know.
3. Get a new hobby or figure out what you're going to do with your time..

Three Action Steps for Your Company:

1. ____

   ____

2. ____

   ____

3. ____

   ____

8

Keeping Your Standards and Procedures Organized

Now let's look at the SOP (Standard Operating Procedures) process as a whole. How do you organize all this stuff so you can find it, use it, and make your business more efficient?

Of course there isn't one perfect way to do things, so I'll just talk a bit about what we do.

First, consider who creates SOPs? Answer: Everyone.

Everyone has duties. The receptionist, the office manager, the bookkeeper, the service coordinator, the technicians, etc. Everyone who does something has to document what they do. Ideally, each person in a role will inherit documentation and procedures. Also ideally, that person will update those procedures. For example, when a web site changes or you switch to a different payroll system, someone needs to update the instructions for payroll.

Maintaining documentation should be a piece of everyone's job description. Employees won't put a priority on it if you don't.

Note: For all documentation, we tend to have one file (one document) for each policy. Yes, you can combine them into a large document, but that's actually harder to manage when it's large and you need to make changes. You might occasionally scoop up all your documentation into a single document, but it is probably easier to manage day-to-day if you keep it in individual files. You can still flag the files with categories and sub-categories in order to make them easier to organize.

Second, consider where you put documentation.

I'm not sure why, but the default answer people want to give is that 1) All documentation should be in the same place, and 2) All documentation should be in some big, electronic thing that's 100% accessible from anywhere on earth. That might work, but we haven't found that approach useful.

Administrative folks use one set of files and folders to do all their work. So we created a "Policies and Procedures" folder within that work area for them. That way, they don't have to go log into some tool they never use. For us, the full path is **x:\Operations\Policies and Procedures**.

Technicians never go there. Why would they? In fact, they don't have permissions to the Operations folder. Technicians have a different place to store stuff: SharePoint. They have an area filled with monthly maintenance checklists, technology SOPs, favorite white papers, New PC checklists, etc. This information is available no matter where the technician is – inside the office or out.

Note: IF your admins use SharePoint all the time already, then keeping their documentation in SharePoint makes sense. But if they never use it for anything else, you're setting yourself up for failure if you ask them to go do this one thing only occasionally.

Third, consider who manages the overall documentation.

At KPEnterprises, this is the service manager. He knows where all the documentation is for admins and for techs. He cleans things up occasionally. If we need to print things out to store in a binder, he does that (but not too often).

The person in charge of documentation is responsible for making sure it's organized and accessible. There's nothing worse than trying to find documentation you KNOW you have, but you don't know where it is.

Documentation naturally divides into two simple categories in the I.T. business: Admin and Tech. But on top of all of that is a third category, Company Policies. Company policies are the "philosophy" topics we've discussed and the SOPs that apply across the board. For example, the philosophy about three-year upgrade cycles (see Volume Three in this SOP book series) and the SOP on Date Formats (see Volume Two in this SOP book series) apply to everyone.

Everyone, especially technicians, needs to know about the philosophy on three-year upgrade cycles. But they don't need to edit it, print it out, or deal with it in any way. Similarly, everyone needs to know and use the approved date formats, but they don't need to edit it.

I prefer to keep these company-wide policies and procedures in with the Admin policies and procedures. These items need their own sub-folder and should only be edited by management types. You won't edit them very often, so it's important that keep them where you can find them!

Finally, consider how you'll backup up all your SOPs.

Ideally, you're already backing up the core data files, and **x:\Operations\Policies and Procedures** is part of that. You'll also need to backup SharePoint, or occasionally do a file/folder copy over to the Operations folder.

Electronic Options

Aside from SharePoint, there are plenty of electronic options for saving all your docs. For us, the PSA system has never been convenient. We used to use ConnectWise. Now we use Autotask. Both are great for time tracking and billing. Both are clunky for things like this. It's just not what they do.

In my opinion, this activity is so straight forward that you just don't need a big database filled with Word and Excel docs in order to organize your documentation.

. . . and you might just decide to keep it all in one big file.

Bottom line: whatever works for you is what you should do. But don't just let everyone put their documentation in whatever folder they feel like. Then it will be lost forever. Whatever you decide to do, you should have a very clear policy about where documentation is located and who uses which system. And this should be so thoroughly embedded into your daily operation that you never have to ask someone to help you find documentation: It will always be in the only place you will ever look.

Don't Delay!

Sometimes we humans put off the things we know we need to do because we're waiting for the "right" solution. In this case that might mean that you delay documenting your operations until you can put it into SharePoint or ConnectWise or Autotask. Or you're waiting for the perfect documentation database to appear.

Don't delay! Go create the folders you need and start putting whatever documentation you already have into those folder.

You already have *some* documentation *somewhere*. Go create an \operations\documentation folder and throw every piece of documentation you can find into it.

That will get you started.

Just as you can't edit a blank page, you can't organize an empty folder. Just get started and then you can make changes and eventually perfect your system.

Three Take-Aways from This Chapter:

1. Each team should have a specific place to store documentation.
2. Documentation should be in the first place you look. If not, it's not in an "obvious" place.
3. Do not delay creating documentation for any reason.

Three Action Steps for Your Company:

1. ______________________________

   ____

2. ______________________________

   ____

3. ______________________________

   ____

9

Team Management of SOPs

One of the most challenging elements of managing documentation with a team is to keep everyone on the same page - so to speak. This is particularly true with processes and procedures. After all, when you create *Your Way* for setting up a machine, you want to make sure that everyone does it *Your Way*!

In terms of "managing" SOPs for your team, there are four primary activities you need to address:

1) Creation of SOPs

2) Changing SOPs

3) Sharing active SOPs (This includes training)

4) Archiving SOPs

1 and 2: Creating and Changing SOPs

The flow chart for all of this is pretty straight forward. Let's say you are going to perform a procedure. First, determine whether there a written procedure already. If yes, execute it. If no, open a template and begin creating the procedure as you execute it. This becomes the first draft of your procedure.

Of course that needs to be stored in an appropriate place so that others can find it, use it, and update it. Thus the procedure becomes a living document. It evolves over time to remain accurate. If it is useful to duplicate this procedure for several clients, then you can create copies that are customized per client. Those are probably stored in individual client folders and not the primary procedure folder.

From time to time procedures become obsolete and are removed from the folders. They should be placed in an archive folder so you can find them if needed, but they are not mixed in with the "live" procedures.

So, from this little narrative, here are the elements you need to create a policy about managing your SOPs. This checklist should be repeated for each team (e.g., finances, sales, tech support):

- Where will the team's SOPs be stored?
- Who is authorized to make changes to procedures (hint: You should justify any answer other than "everyone")
- The last item in every checklist or procedure should be "Update this document"

3 and 4: Sharing and Archiving SOPs

Sharing includes putting things where you can find them AND training employees to use the SOPs. These are both much easier if you have regular employee meetings - such as a regular Monday morning huddle. Sharing includes making sure everyone knows whether they'll find what they're looking for on the SharePoint site, the company's public folder, inside Evernote, etc.

Training is critically important. With every process, every procedure, and every checklist, you should make sure that everyone on the team is executing well. That means that they watch someone execute the procedure, then someone watches them execute. Only then are they allowed to execute on their own.

If a procedure is new to the team, the team should go through it together to make sure all questions are answered. This is particularly important if a task used to be reserved for one or two high-level technicians and now everyone on the team is going to perform that task.

Training is also important as your team grows. From time to time it is useful to go through even mundane procedures and make sure everyone knows Your Way of doing things.

Finally, someone on each team needs to be responsible for weeding out old procedures. These might be obsolete (such as testing the backup tapes) or something that is now performed per-client so a universal procedure is no longer relevant. In some cases, you might have a folder for templates that are personalized for each client.

Never simply delete old procedures. Move them to the archive folder. You never know what you're going to need some day!

The SOP Mentality

This seems like a lot of activity around SOPs. Just keep it in perspective: This is a lot of activity around standardization of your company. It's a lot of activity around doing things the right way. It's a culture that focuses a little bit every day on the things that will make your company systematically successful!

You **brand** – Your Way – literally defines your company. When employees do things consistently, that builds your brand identity. When everyone knows Your Way, that builds brand identity. When everyone supports each other in doing things Your Way, that builds brand identity.

This is not an intellectual exercise in organizing papers or wasting time. This is about building a strong, successful organization.

Three Take-Aways from This Chapter:

1. You need processes for creating, changing, sharing, and archiving SOPs.
2. Every single employee needs to learn these processes.
3. You build your brand by building consistent SOPs.

Three Action Steps for Your Company:

1. ____

   ____

2. ____

   ____

3. ____

   ____

10

Making Exceptions to SOPs

You might be surprised to hear me say this, but there are lots of exceptions to the rules. Well, to some rules. There are built-in exceptions, emergency exceptions, bad habit exceptions, and common sense exceptions. There are also different kinds of SOPs. Some SOPs must be followed exactly and perfectly each time and some are much more flexible.

First, let's talk about those internal to your company. Then we'll look at how you manage exceptions with clients.

In the big picture, common sense is the most important piece of all of this. SOPs exist to make life easier. Well, life and work. When SOPs get in the way of smooth and efficient operations, then need to be set aside. We'll come back to this.

Built-In Exceptions to SOPs

Some SOPs work best if you can build in the exceptions. For example, we have a very strong policy of working from highest to lowest priority. We don't want people wasting time working on Low-Priority activities when High-Priority activities can be moved forward. Further, we have a well-defined process that says that all service tickets are worked from highest to lowest priority. BUT . . .

We also have a built-in exception to this rule.

When I go to a client's office, I start by looking at all the open tickets they have. If I'm going to go onsite, I will try to knock out all the tickets I can in the time allotted. I'm not going to take care of one high priority item, bill them for an hour, and then leave. In addition to being less efficient in the long run, that would be pretty bad customer service.

So I try to get as many tickets completed as possible. In particular, I make sure that the tasks that require an on-site technician are completed.

This built-in exception makes sure that I give good service. It also makes sure that we address all those medium and low priority service tickets that might not otherwise get any attention.

When you create built-in exceptions, make sure they actually add value to what you're doing. I think the example here is perhaps the most important built-in exception we have. It truly improves our process in several ways.

Emergency Exceptions and Bad Habit Exceptions

Emergency exceptions to SOPs should be rare (of course). Sometimes you just need to cut through the red tape – even if you created the red tape. The problem is that this decision is so subjective. You get to decide what's an emergency. If you're the owner, you don't really have to justify it to anyone.

It is a bad habit to start making exceptions and excuses. Once you go down that road, every day is a series of exceptions to the rules. Pretty soon there's no point in having SOPs at all.

The most common "excuse" given for breaking SOPs is that it's faster to "just do it" rather than follow the established process. It's very much like hiring an employee and then doing all the work yourself because it's faster than training them how to do it. You know intellectually that it's better in the long run to follow the SOP (or train the employee). But right now, today, with this one little task, it's faster to just do it.

The bottom line here is discipline.

I will say: Having employees helps. The favorite employee past time is watching the boss. So if the boss cuts corners, the employees know it's okay to cut corners. Employees will keep you in line. And they will support each other.

Once you have established SOPs and everyone is trained, then you should have the discussion about exceptions. Think of it this way: Once you know all the rules, you can make good decisions about when to break them. But that doesn't change the fact that the rules still need to be followed.

Letting Clients Make Exceptions

Client related policies and procedures are a little different. For example, it's easy to say that you have to change your password every 30 days, but many clients simply refuse to follow this. So where do you stand firm and where do you let the client make the rules?

You probably have very few technology-related rules that you impose on your clients. You ask them to switch the backup discs or tapes; you ask them to change their passwords; you ask them to log off at night but leave the machines on; etc. A few very reasonable suggestions.

In fact, every "policy" you give them is either 1) For their own good, or 2) Related to doing business with you.

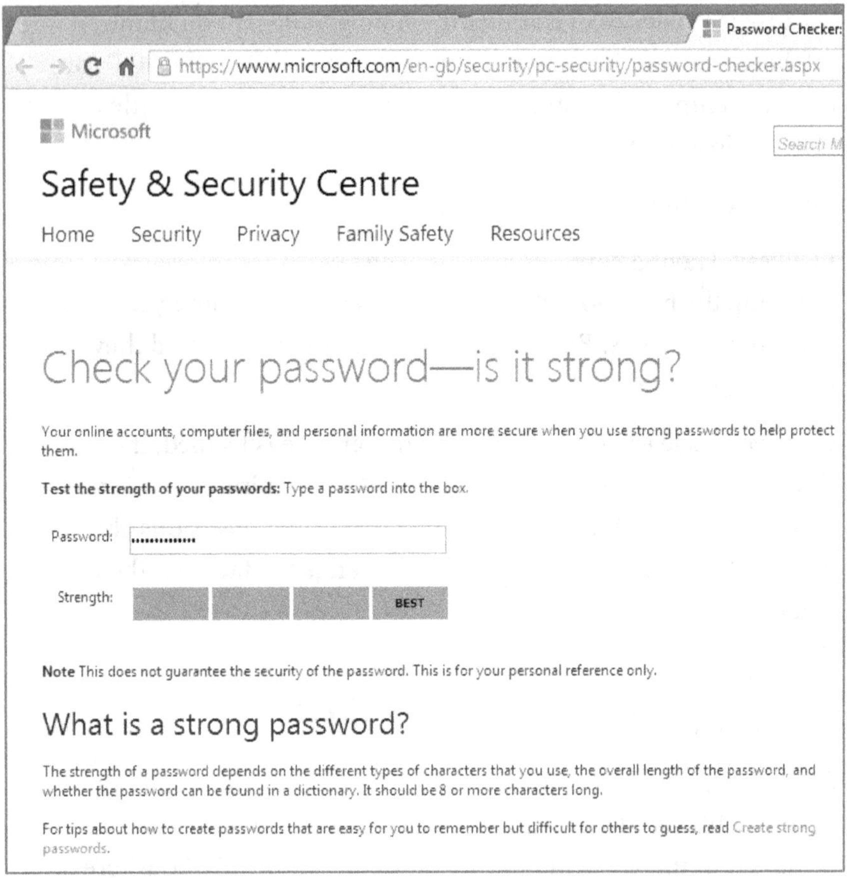

Password Checker:

https://www.microsoft.com/en-gb/security/pc-security/password-checker.aspx

Microsoft

Search M

Safety & Security Centre

Home Security Privacy Family Safety Resources

Check your password—is it strong?

Your online accounts, computer files, and personal information are more secure when you use strong passwords to help protect them.

Test the strength of your passwords: Type a password into the box.

Password: ••••••••••••••

Strength: BEST

Note This does not guarantee the security of the password. This is for your personal reference only.

What is a strong password?

The strength of a password depends on the different types of characters that you use, the overall length of the password, and whether the password can be found in a dictionary. It should be 8 or more characters long.

For tips about how to create passwords that are easy for you to remember but difficult for others to guess, read Create strong passwords.

https://www.microsoft.com/en-gb/security/pc-security/password-checker.aspx

When it comes to doing things that are in their own interest, you have very little control. You can educate them, remind them, and warn them. But at the end of the day, you can't care more about their network than they do. So if they don't tend to the backup drives, there's very little you can do.

You should protect yourself when clients make certain bad decisions. For example, if a client will not take steps to make sure that they change passwords or backup their data, you need to let them know - in writing - that you can't be responsible for these things.

At the end of the day, the best you can do is to make good recommendations and encourage the client to take your advice. But if they don't want to follow your advice, there's not much you can do.

Who Can Make Exceptions?

You have to decide who can make exceptions to SOPs within your company and at the client's office. Within your company, this list should be rather limited. Maybe the owner and the Service Manager. Every person who wants to make an exception should be required to contact the one or two people who can authorize an exception.

At the client, it's a similar thing. Once you and the client have established some rules, you should also decide when they can be broken. Owners and partners usually exclude themselves. But they don't want everyone to have that power.

Meet with the client and decide who can make exceptions before an exception is needed.

Three Take-Aways from This Chapter:

1. Determine who can make exceptions to your SOPs. It shouldn't be everyone.
2. Monitor your exceptions and keep them under control.
3. You can't care more about the client's systems than they do.

Three Action Steps for Your Company:

1. ______________________________

   ____

2. ______________________________

   ____

3. ______________________________

   ____

11

Rules for Working at Home

There are two primary times when an MSP will work from home. The first is when you have no other office. This might be because you're just starting out, you have no employees, or your employees or contractors also work at home. The second is when you get larger and choose to work at home in order to increase productivity or work on special projects. Or you might be an employee working from home for the same reasons.

In either case, here are some tips for working at home in order to be as productive as possible.

Have a Good Home Work Environment

The first thing you need to do if you're working at home is to set up an actual office – a place to work. When I first started my business, I was worried about taking the home office deduction. My accountant looked at my office and said I had nothing to worry about. The reason was simple: That room was filled with work things – a long table for building PCs, a desk, shelves full of computer books, and a file cabinet.

It was obviously an office and not a bedroom.

(Side note: Talk to your tax adviser. I am not one. But I believe you cannot take a home office deduction if you have someplace else to work, such as an office space.)

Tax considerations aside, your home office should be designed and organized to be as productive as possible. That means you need a good desk, a good chair, a good PC, a good phone, etc. You need all the office basics so that you don't spend your home office time running to Staples or Kinko's. Good furniture will also allow you to be comfortable, which will improve productivity.

Your home office should also have clear boundaries. Even if you have to set up shop in the family room or kitchen (not recommended), you need to have a place that is "yours" and off limits to the rest of the family. this also helps you set the interruption boundaries discussed below.

Even if you're the "messy desk" type, your home office desk should have a nice clear area to get work done. Again, the goal is to create a productive environment.

Have Good Home Work Habits

There are two sets of work habits related to working at home successfully. The first has to do with the "home" part of the equation. The second are rules you should follow at the office and keep following when you work from home.

Perhaps the most important habit for working at home is to pretend you're at the office. That means you **dress for work**. Even though we joke about working in your pajamas, don't do it. Put on your uniform – a nice pair of pants and a business casual shirt.

Dressing for work puts you in the right mind set. That's huge for developing the self-discipline you need to work from home.

It is also important to **set work hours** and take them seriously. The flexibility of working from home means that you might start a little later or earlier than normal. But whatever hours you set, stick to them! Pretend you are clocking in and clocking out. In between is work.

When you work, work. No visits to the kitchen. No TV. No chores. No "home" paperwork. These can be big temptations, especially if that desk is the same place you work on home finances.

You need your family to support your home work limits. That means **they can't interrupt you** at your home office any more than they interrupt you at your other office. You might accomplish this by closing the door, setting out orange cones, or putting up a sign. Whatever works for you is fine.

This can be very difficult, but you need to be diligent enforcing this. It will take time for the family to get used to this, but they will.

Then there are rules you should follow at any office, so don't lose these good habits just because you're working at home:

- **No interruptions** during working hours! Do not be interrupt-driven. Focus on what you're doing. Do it well, then move to the next task.
- **Take breaks.** You simply cannot work eight hours straight without a break. If you do, you will find that you are less productive. Take a break or two in the morning and at least two in the afternoon. And of course you should stop for lunch. This is the only time you can violate the "no kitchen" rule.

Be sure to keep the breaks to 5-10 minutes and lunch to an hour. Don't get side tracked with a television show, video game, etc. For my breaks, I stand up and listen to one or two songs on the stereo. That's at least five minutes. It gets my circulation going, and then I return to work refreshed.

- Check out at 5PM and **stop working**!
- **Track your time** completely and accurately. That means you need to track what you're doing from 8AM to 5PM (or whatever your hours are). If you have a PSA, use it from home. There's no excuse to stop using your PSA to enter time just because you are at home.

Working Effectively with Employees or Contractors from Home

One final note. If you do have employees or contractors you need to work with, you need to make time to actually meet with them. Totally virtual businesses are hard to maintain. Some human contact is needed.

When I started having employees, I had them come to my house. But that quickly became inconvenient for everyone. So I scheduled meetings at local coffee shops or restaurants. That worked much better. And, of course, when that didn't work anymore it was because we really did need to get an office.

When employees work from home they need to understand that this is a privilege that is granted with the understanding that they will be as productive at home as they are at work. Having a PSA makes this much easier to manage. But no matter how your company is organized, home workers need to produce the same results as they would in the office.

For many companies, allowing employees to work from home builds a stronger team. It shows you trust them, it reduces their commute, and it shows that the company is flexible. It also allows employees to take care of sick kids or other family matters while still getting their work done. That kind work/life balance is good for everyone.

I cannot explain why Yahoo stopped letting employees work from home. Done right it is one of the best things you can do for your company.

Three Take-Aways from This Chapter:

1. Set up a dedicated space for your office.
2. Set work hours and enforce them strictly.
3. Dress for success.

Three Action Steps for Your Company:

1. ______________________________

   ____

2. ______________________________

   ____

3. ______________________________

   ____

12

Phone Etiquette and Procedures

Let me start with a disclaimer: I used to be addicted to the telephone. Now I rarely use it except to record podcasts. At the same time, many clients love the telephone. For some reason, it makes them feel like they're getting speedy service, even when entering a service ticket is always a faster way to get service (See the chapters "Clients Who Abuse the Phones" later in this book and "How Do Service Requests Get Into Your System?" in Volume Four of this book series).

Nevertheless . . .

People will call your business. Clients, vendors, strangers, sales people, etc. Very often, you know who's calling because of Caller ID, but not always. Most of these rules apply whether you know the caller or not. There's one exception, and it's spelled out.

The most important rule about phones is related to one of the most important rules about running your business: **Don't be interrupt-driven**. Focus on the job in front of you.

Most people consider it rude to turn away from someone while in a conversation and give all your attention to someone else. But somehow we think it's okay to do this when the phone rings.

No matter what you're doing, your attention should be *there* – in the present moment. You should not stop doing something just because the phone rings. Focus on the thing you're doing. Do it well. Let the system work. When you're done with the job in front of you, then use the system to see what the next most important thing is.

(On focus, please see my book *Relax Focus Succeed* and *The Power of Focus* by Jack Canfield.)

So we have rules about phone usage. Many of them assume that you have accepted the Standard Operating Procedure of not allowing yourself and your employees to be interrupt-driven. Remember, the goal of these SOPs is to make your business work better. That means making more money, providing better service, and making your clients happier.

As always, adjust for your own business practices.

Note: The remainder of this discussion assumes that we are talking about a managed service business and NOT a "help desk." If you have a help desk, it is intended to respond to interruptions. I would argue that your help desk should work exactly the same, except that you would guarantee that a human answers the phone. Once a ticket is created, you would simply channel "help desk" calls into the help desk queue.

As you will see, these rules are deeply integrated into the other SOPs of your business. These include client communications, time management, etc.

General Rules

- Telephones are answered by the office manager (a non-technical person)
- If the office manager is not available, the service manager or service coordinator answers the phone
- Technicians do not answer any phones at any time unless it is one of your co-workers or it is identifiable as being directly related to the Service Request or Activity you are working on at the time
- Whoever answers the phone may:
  1. Create a new service request
  2. Update a new service request
  3. Transfer the phone to the service manager, if appropriate
  4. Transfer the phone to voice mail, if appropriate

The most common result will be that a new service ticket will be created, or that an existing service ticket will be updated with notes. I point that out because **interrupting technicians** is NOT a common event.

- If no one is available to answer the phone, the call is routed to the Service Manager or Service Coordinator's phone. If that is not answered, it rolls to voicemail. As a result, that person will need to check voicemail on a regular basis.
- Personal phone calls are made during break times and if necessary in between service calls. They should not be made in the middle of billable time.
- Always set phones to the lowest audible setting (or vibrate) when in any office, including at our own

- Do not answer your desk or cell phone when you are in a meeting or giving someone else your attention
- Try to check voice mail every other hour on the hour for best response time. A simple rule is every odd hour of the day. This allows for a check after lunch and as one of the last things in the day.
- No personal phone calls while on clients site ever!
- DO NOT give out personal cell phone numbers
- Clients should always call your primary phone number for technical support

Resetting the Interrupt

It is a fact that, at one time or another, you will find yourself on the phone with a client who needs attention but you cannot give it to them for one reason or another. The acceptable phrases to memorize and use are:

- "I'm going to help you get a Service Request put into the system so that the service manager can get it prioritized and get someone on it as soon as possible."
- "Even though you have reached me directly I am currently on another task / working with another client and can't change my focus. I'm going to help you . . ." (see text above)

Voice Mail

Your desk phones and cell phones should have a standardized message and guide people to follow your company processes for fastest support.

Here's a sample to get you started:

“Hello. You have reached the voice mail for Jane Technician. Please leave me a detailed message and I will return your call as soon as possible. If this is an urgent issue, please call the xxx-xxxx extension 1 for the Service Manager."

Implementation Notes

There's a lot here.

Implementing these phone rules consists of a few simple steps:

1. Define your rules. Write then down and document them.
2. Train your staff. Give them written copies of these procedures.
3. Expect all personnel to follow the procedures. Support each other in following these procedures.

Benefits

These rules do not exist for arbitrary reasons. They should be formulated to enforce the **profitable** operation of your company.

More than almost any other tool at your disposal, the telephone can interrupt your people and your processes very quickly and repeatedly. If you're not familiar with *First Things First* by Steven Covey, et al., it is definitely worth your while.

One of the key lessons of that book is to learn the difference between **Important** and **Urgent**. Telephone calls can easily seem to be urgent. That doesn't make them important.

When phone communications are not important, then they need to be controlled, no matter how "urgent" they seem.

As a result, you need to craft telephone rules that keep your people on track, efficient, and profitable.

Success Is In The Follow-Up

Telephone communications are extremely important. So don't ignore them. This policy is not intended to lower your service level. It is intended to improve you current service (whatever you're working on when the phone rings) and help you make more money.

Because we have been programmed to drop everything instantly when we hear a phone ring, you need to really train your employees about this. Let them know that everyone is following the same rules.

As strange as it sounds, the interruption reflex is so strong with phones that people will feel anxiety about not answering them. You may not even believe that it's okay to turn off your ringer.

My ringer is almost never on. Sometimes it goes on and up after I use my GPS navigator. Then when my phone rings, I look around and wonder what that sound is. Even my marketing manager has been known to ask me, "What is that?" when my phone rings.

Remember that you are NOT ignoring the phone or the client. You are managing your communications. See the next two chapters.

Three Take-Aways from This Chapter:

1. Do not let phone calls interrupt you.
2. Create policies so that everyone knows it is okay to ignore the phones.
3. DO follow up on every phone call in a timely manner.

Three Action Steps for Your Company:

1. ____________________

   ____

2. ____________________

   ____

3. ____________________

   ____

13

Telephone Philosophy and General Rules

Phones are a tough topic. When you're really small (1-2 person shop), you probably forward everything to your cell phone and probably answer it all the time. When you get an voice mail you call someone back immediately.

That's a very natural thing to do. It's very personal and gives clients a strong sense of being served.

BUT . . . This behavior can also lead to too much interruption and habits that do not serve you well in the long run. In general, you should not have any processes that allow people to simply interrupt what you're doing and reset your productivity. This chapter covers some general rules for success with the phones. The next chapter covers "How Much Interruption is Okay?"

Phones and Phone Etiquette

Here are the proposed guidelines. Consider this a draft SOP:

Philosophy

It has been set out that this company will not be interrupt driven by phones of any type. It is considered rude to turn away from someone while in a conversation only to give all your attention to another. Many people today do this when their phone rings, but we will not.

It is also recognized that anyone working on a task is distracted from that task the second they change their focus to the phone. This can be an almost addictive, compulsive behavior.

Personal phone calls should be attended to during break times and if necessary in between service calls in such a manner that they do not interrupt the flow of work.

It is assumed you prioritize your personal and work life in some organized fashion so that higher priority items and addressed before lower priority items, and that there is a process for putting on your "to do" list.

General Rules

- Technicians do not answer any phones at any time unless it is one of your co-workers or it is identifiable as being directly related to the Service Request or Activity you are working on at the time.
- Always set phones to lowest audible setting (or vibrate) when in any office including our own.
- Do not answer your desk or cell phone when you are in a meeting or giving someone else your attention.
- Try to check voice mail every other hour on the hour for best response time. A simple rule is every odd hour of the day.

This allows for a check after lunch and as one of the last things in the day.

- No personal phone calls while on client sites ever!

Voice Mail

- Desk Phones have programmed voice mail greetings and menus.
- Desk phone voice mail passwords are set to the norm defined in the company policy.
- All voice mail greetings must closely resemble the following statement and must contain the same information:

"Hello you have reached the voice mail for Jane Technician. Please leave me a detailed message and I will return your call as soon as possible. If this is of an urgent nature, please call the 916-555-1212 extension 1 for the Service Manager."

Implications

Phones are an interesting thing. Somehow, our society has come to believe that you should answer the phone as soon as it rings. I've been in sales meetings when a cell phone rings. Invariable, the prospect will say "Do you want to get that?" No. In fact, the person with the phone should have put it on silent or left it in the car.

When you are talking to someone on the phone, they deserve your full attention. When you're talking to someone in person (even a fellow employee), they deserve your full attention. But more than that: Your company is less productive and more stressful when it's filled with interruptions.

Here's a little snippet from some scientific research:

"When people are constantly interrupted, they develop a mode of working faster (and writing less) to compensate for the time they know they will lose by being interrupted. Yet working faster with interruptions has its cost: people in the interrupted conditions experienced a higher workload, more stress, higher frustration, more time pressure, and effort. So interrupted work may be done faster, but at a price."

The Cost of Interrupted Work: More Speed and Stress by Gloria Mark, Department of Informatics, University of California, Irvine and Daniela Gudith and Ulrich Klocke, Institute of Psychology, Humboldt University, Berlin, Germany.

See http://www.ics.uci.edu/~gmark/chi08-mark.pdf

With phones, our big fear is that we'll give a bad customer service response. But, really, we find that 99% of clients are perfectly happy if they get a reasonable response. In our modern world, voice mail and call-backs are common. If you have ways for clients to enter service tickets by phone, email, and web portal, then it's up to you to respond in a timely fashion. In general, if you get back within an hour, they're happy.

If a client has a true emergency, then you need to simply follow the processes we've outlined already. Interrupting your business does not automatically mean better service for the client.

Implementation

Implementing this policy is pretty simple. You should write up a brief description of the procedure and put it into your SOP binder. Distribute it to your staff. Maybe hold a meeting to discuss this policy and commit to it.

This kind of policy requires that everyone on the team

1) Be aware of the policy

2) Practice the policy

3) Correct one another's errors

4) Support one another with reminders

Three Take-Aways from This Chapter:

1. Allowing interruptions will create a more stressful and less productive environment.
2. Create a standardized policy and distribute it.
3. Everyone on your team should support each other in this.

Three Action Steps for Your Company:

1. ______________________________

 ____

2. ______________________________

 ____

3. ______________________________

 ____

14

How Much Interruption is Okay?

In the last two chapters we've talked about not being controlled by your telephone. It's okay to call people back. Just make sure you do it in a timely manner!

But interruptions do happen. Now, what do you do to deal with the interruption? It is a fact that at one time or another you will find yourself on the phone with a client who needs attention but you cannot give it to them for one reason or another. The acceptable phrases are given above.

You can limit interruptions by having a well thought-out phone tree. That means:

1) DO NOT give out personal cell phone numbers. Period.

2) Clients should always call the main phone number. Press "1" for tech support. That might go to your cell phone, but the client needs to call the main number!

3) After hours, the phone tree automatically rolls to an after-hours message. If the client has an urgent matter, they can leave a message. You'll get a page/text and you can call them back.

You never need to answer the phone after hours. If your clients consistently call you during evenings and weekends, it's because you have trained them to do so. Stop it. You'll be amazed at how easily they comply. Why? Because you are one of only two vendors that DON'T have a policy about this.

Note: Of course you should be reading this within the context of the entire 4-book series. That means you should have a **process** for handling service calls, getting service requests into your system, etc.

Interruptions Kill Business

I harp on this because we live in a society that believes you can do multiple things at once. You can't. Period. I know people can point to articles debating this philosophically. But **empirically**, human beings cannot multi-task. Human beings can **switch between tasks**. Sometimes they can do it very fast. But you can't do two things at once.

So . . . you're working and you get interrupted. What effect does that have on your performance?

The research is pretty amazing, but not very widely publicized. I guess we don't want to hear that our constant interruptions are bad. We enjoy them!

In many cases, we are happy to be interrupted. That's fine. But accept to yourself that that's what you're doing. If you DON'T want to be interrupted, then you need to put in systems to reduce interruptions.

Here's an interesting bit of research:

"We found about 82 percent of all interrupted work is resumed on the same day. But here's the bad news – it it takes an average of 23 minutes and 15 seconds to get back to the task." See *Worker, Interrupted: The Cost of Task Switching* (http://www.fastcompany.com/articles/2008/07/interview-gloria-mark.html).

Other research found the interruption to be more like 15 minutes. But still, that's huge.

One estimate is that the average knowledge worker loses more than $10,000/year in productive labor due to interruptions. See http://www.slate.com/articles/news_and_politics/hey_wait_a_minute/2006/03/workus_interruptus.html.

It's Not Just Phones

Phones are the most obvious examples of interruptions, but there are plenty more. People walk into each others' work space and just start talking – without any regard for what the other person is doing. Outlook and AOL and a hundred other programs beep and tweet and pop up on your screen.

Stop it.

Don't let other people do it.

Have a philosophy of non-interruption.

Develop work processes, procedures, and policies that weed out interruptions and encourage solid work habits.

Elsewhere we'll talk about priorities. But just consider this. If you are always working on the highest priority task available to you, then there is almost zero probability that the interruption will be a higher priority. So don't feel bad about not allowing the interruption.

In the log I discuss below, make special note of the priority of interruptions. Most phone calls are extremely low priority. On an average day I will miss between five and ten phone calls because my phone is off or in another room. It is rare that anyone leaves a voicemail because the call was unimportant in the first place!

Keep a Log

Try this and see for yourself how often you are affected by interruptions: **Keep a Log**. Just like a food log for dieters. Log the date, time, and a quick note about the interruption. Then, at the end of the day, evaluate whether the interruption was High, Medium, or Low priority. Then estimate how long the interruption affected your work.

Keep a total every day for one week. I'll bet you have more than ten interruptions per day. At six minutes (interruption + time to get back on task), that's one hour per day. When I did this, many years ago, the total was more than 20/day. Now I'm pretty brutal about not being interrupt-driven.

You should always work from highest to lowest priority. Working on something just because you are interrupted means that you totally ignore the priority system! That's being interrupt-driven.

Implementation

To implement this policy, start by writing up a general policy (1-2 paragraphs). Then begin building systems (like using your PSA properly and creating a working phone tree).

This kind of policy requires that everyone on the team

1) Be aware of the policy

2) Practice the policy

3) Correct one another's errors

4) Support one another with reminders

Three Take-Aways from This Chapter:

1. Keep an "Interruption Diet" log.
2. Accept that you cannot multi-task and focus your attention on the job in front of you.
3. Work from highest priority to lowest priority – and keep interruptions where they belong.

Three Action Steps for Your Company:

1. ______________________________

   ____

2. ______________________________

   ____

3. ______________________________

   ____

15

Signing Service Agreements

I've written hundreds of pages on service agreements. In fact, I wrote a book on them! This chapter is not about all about WHY you need service agreements or WHAT they need to look like. This post is very simply about a policy THAT you will have service agreements with every single client. As with all policies, it moves from a general principle to a process, procedures, and checklists. Se the discussion of this in Chapter One.

Your Policy: Everyone Signs a Service Agreement

As a starting point, let's just adopt the policy stated above: Everyone we do work for must have some kind of signed agreement for services. Great.

Now, there are different types of service agreements. The most basic is a 1-2 page "terms of service" agreement. You might also have agreements for basic break/fix, managed services, blocks of time, projects, etc. You might have one agreement flexible enough to be used for all of these.

So, to implement your policy, you first need to have one or more service agreements that people can sign. Then you need a policy that says that everyone should sign. Finally, you need processes and procedures, and even a checklist, to make sure this happens.

See the chapter "Setting Up a New Managed Service Client (Checklist)" in Volume Three of this book series.

All of that happens as soon as the client signs a service agreement. Well, at least when they sign a managed services agreement. When you go through that checklist, I hope you can see that there's a lot of time (and a little money) involved in setting up a new M.S. client. So they better be under contract.

As for simple break/fix and small jobs, you will need a different process. Once you have the policy in place that everyone must have an agreement, you need to figure out how you'll make that happen. As a rule, larger agreements for ongoing service involve some kind of sales process that concludes with a signed agreement.

Smaller projects require just the 1-2 page "terms of service" agreement. In our company, the owner or service manager generally works these jobs so they can meet the client and determine whether we want to pursue an ongoing relationship with them. The owner or service manager simply takes the 1-2 page "terms of service" agreement with him and has the prospect sign it before anything else is done.

If a technician is sent to do the job, the process is basically the same. They carry copies of the 1-2 page "terms of service" agreement and ask the prospect to sign it. Technicians need to be very clear on this point: No work can be done before that agreement is signed. Period.

This policy is pretty simple and straight forward. You can adopt it in sixty seconds and then simply do it from now on. Implementation simply consists of writing a quick process for writing up each kind of agreement. Assuming an agreement is the end product of a sales call, the only real procedure you need is about the terms of service agreement.

Just do it.

Three Take-Aways from This Chapter:

1. All work must be performed within a Service Agreement of some kind.
2. It's a good idea to have the owner or service manager perform the first job with a new client.
3. Simple "terms of service" agreements can be executed by any technician.

Three Action Steps for Your Company:

1. ________________________________

   ____

2. ________________________________

   ____

3. ________________________________

   ____

Section II

The Central Role of Finance

16

Building a Business Plan for Your I.T. Company

Nobody wants to fail, but very few people plan to succeed.

Let's start out with a reality check: Most really smart business owners don't think they need a business plan. Their business is working fine and they know they can get up every day and do it again. The problem is: That behavior got them "here" and will keep them right where they are.

In 2013 I had three coaching clients who were planning to move themselves, their businesses, and their families from one state to another. That takes planning. That takes money. That takes a plan to make sure you don't skip a beat.

Your goals may not be as clear or as big of a challenge. But you should have goals for yourself and your business. You should also have a quick sketch of where your business has been and where it is going.

And your business should operate perfectly consistently with your goals.

I believe that any IT consultant who has gross revenue under $150,000 can double that top line revenue in 12 months. And you don't have to be a super salesman. And you don't have to give up your personal life.

What you DO have to do is to make a plan!

You'll have to work hard. But once you set your sights on a specific goal, you can achieve it. You'll have to make some strategic decisions. You'll have to take some chances. And you'll have to deliver what you sell. But in the days of managed services, you should be able to manage a lot of workstations and servers by yourself. Adding a dozen more clients will require some help. But that's part of the plan.

Back in 2008 I wrote a five-part blog series on creating your business plan for the new year. You can find those articles in the electronic contents for this book series. Just register your book at www.smbbooks.com. The five part series is called "Business Plan in a Month."

I'm not going to repeat all that here, but focus on the Process of creating a business plan.

Now, if you want a little assist with this project, you might also try *Business Plan Pro* software (www.paloalto.com/business_plan_software). I have used Business Plan Pro. I'm not sure I'd endorse it. After all, it is basically a tool that interviews you and has you do some busy work. When you're done, you get a kludgy business plan, but at least you have one!

For a different approach, you should also take a look at *The One Page Business Plan* product (www.onepagebusinessplan.com/books2.htm). Again, just a tool that might be helpful.

Motivation is the killer when it comes to business plans. Everyone says they want to, but don't know how to start. All I can recommend is that you make a commitment and spend a tiny bit of time each day. Don't try to tackle the whole thing in one weekend.

As for excuses: You DO have the time. This time is an investment that will free up lots of time in the future. You DO know how. A business plan is extremely simple. It has a quick look back, a somewhat thoughtful look forward, some goals, and a statement of why you're in business.

Your business plan might not be one page, but it can be extremely small. I revise mine every year and it's eight pages - six of those are financial printouts. I print out P&L (profit and loss) reports for the last three years and the next three years.

When you boil a business plan down to its absolute basics, it needs to contain just a few things:

- Where we are and how we got here
- Where we're going (overall goals) and how we'll get there

Each of these has a finance component, which can be very simple.

Free Handout for Building Your IT Business Plan

I've created a simple Excel spreadsheet you can use as a starting place if you don't already have one. Again, it's part of the downloads for this book series. Just register your book.

You'll get a zip file with an Excel spreadsheet and three PDF documents (the three pages of the Excel spreadsheet. Poke around and play with that spreadsheet. Make a copy for your own company so you can always go back to the original and look at formulas, etc.

I discuss that spreadsheet in some detail in the longer blog posts mentioned earlier.

So that's the piece that will get you started on the financial side. But a business plan is a lot more than that. I always tell my coaching clients: Your business exists to help you reach your personal goals. That's what small business is all about.

So you can't just go to work every day and do what you did yesterday. You need to make decisions based on whether they advance your goals - business and personal. This is an extremely powerful way to look at the world!

I ask you to take this seriously. Take 15-20 minutes every day to stop and think about your personal and professional lives. Sounds simple, but it's not. The hardest part is sitting down to do this.

If you can fill out this tiny form with meaningful answers, you've got a business plan:

1. What is your company mission statement

2. What are your three primary goals for the next calendar quarter?

a.

b.

c.

3. What are your three primary goals for the year as a whole?

a.

b.

c.

Do not do this fast. Work on it every day and review over and over. Don't do hasty goal-setting in the week between Christmas and New Years. Goal-setting is arguably the most important thing in your life, and your business.

You can absolutely reach your goals - if you have a plan. No one stumbles their way to amazing achievements. (Yeah, bring up some one in a billion exception. But we both know that my point is still valid.)

If you don't have a plan to convert to managed services, it won't happen. If you don't have a plan to formulate your cloud service offering, it won't happen. If you don't have a plan to get ten new clients, it won't happen. If you don't have a plan to double your revenue, it won't happen.

You get the point.

So go get a tiny little 1/2" binder and print out the pieces you have:

- A Mission Statement
- Three specific, measurable goals for the next quarter
- Three specific, measurable goals for the next year
- Financial overview for the last three years
- Very rough first take on projected financials for the next three years

The easiest part should be the financial reports. Oddly enough, most people set up their goals next (quarterly and yearly). But you really need to start with the mission statement.

Why, why, why, why, why are you doing any of this?

Building Future Business Plans

The really good news is that next year's business plan will be a lot easier to complete. Your past financials will simply move up a year. The projections for the next three years will be a little clearer after you spend a year with a plan.

And your mission statement probably won't change much year to year. If it does, you need to spend more quiet time fine-tuning your personal and business goals. Mission statements should be long term commitments about WHY your business exists.

So that leaves goals. As you can imagine, you're going to need to set up new goals each quarter to keep that piece current. And after a year, you'll see how quarterly goals roll up into your annual goals. It's like steering a ship. No matter how big the ship, you can move it a little at a time until it's heading where you want.

Motivation Again

I've worked with thousands of business owners over the years. People have a hard time just getting started with this. I don't know how to make you stop and do this.

Maybe you need to get one or two friends together and commit to each other that you'll build business plans in a month. In fact, you can then help review each other's plans for a "reality check" on numbers and goals.

I really believe this is approximately the most important thing you need to do right now. Everything else, no matter how important it is, is pointless unless it advances your mission and goals. And you might have a gut feeling about your mission and goals, but that's pretty vague.

If you can't articulate WHAT you want to do and HOW you're doing to do it, then you need to keep polishing the business plan.

A partner of some kind is extremely helpful here. It could be a spouse, an employee, or another business owner. Anyone who is willing to help will do. Explain to that person what you want to do with your business and why you want to do it. They need to be totally honest with you. If you can successfully describe these things to someone else, then you have a plan.

Write it down and make it happen!

Three Take-Aways from This Chapter:

1. Nothing happens by itself. Make a plan.
2. Find an accountability partner and help each other build business plans.
3. Explore the articles and tools out there – but don't delay because you're doing research!

Three Action Steps for Your Company:

1. ______________________________

   ____

2. ______________________________

   ____

3. ______________________________

   ____

17

Billing Procedures and Policies

Prelude to the Policy: Before you get down to sending out invoices, you need to be very rigorous about getting the right information into your PSA (professional services automation tool). For example, you need to be sure about what's Included and Excluded from managed services. Which is to say, what's Billable and Unbillable. Even within "covered" service requests there can be billable time entries.

Review your time entries against your policies about on site and off site labor as well as normal hours vs. after-hours rates. In all cases you need to keep track of your minimum charges. You also need to apply any credits or write-offs.

In other words: GIGO - Garbage In, Garbage Out. You can't get out of the system something you haven't put into the system.

You need rigorous procedures to make sure all the time entries in all the tickets are correct. Then you can proceed to the billing process.

See the chapter "Invoice Review and Processing."

Invoicing

You basically have three times when you invoice clients. First, you invoice for monthly services such as managed services, BDR, hosted exchange, etc. Second, you have project labor that might be billed in advance, weekly, or monthly. Third, you will have product purchases such as hardware and software.

The chapter on “Invoice Review and Processing” walkw through the process of cleaning up time entries and invoicing for periodic labor. Other invoicing is similar. You need to decide whether you want to run all billing through the PSA or deal with it separately. "Separately" might mean a quoting tool such as QuoteWerks or Quosal, or it might simply be QuickBooks.

But what are your billing policies?

For most of us, our policies just evolved over time. They may not be coherent. We may have different policies for different clients. Obviously, you can predict what I'm going to say next. You need a small set of consistent policies about how you bill and when you bill. Let's take the three categories one at a time.

But first . . .

Get Paid in Advance!

Let me preface this by saying that we get prepaid for 98% of everything. Everything. Period. I get lots of push-back from consultants who have convinced themselves that they cannot get paid in advance. "My clients wouldn't do that. They'd go somewhere else. They'll leave me."

Not true. Not true. Not true. With VERY few exceptions, most clients will simply comply. If you feel like you have to make excuses, blame the economy, your supplies, the bank, or me. But just write a memo and be done with it. Think of all the things you pay in advance. Your clients are the same way. Don't have both sides of the conversation!

Billing Policies for Monthly Recurring Charges

Proposed policy: All monthly recurring charges must be paid in advance by credit card or ACH on the first day of the month.

That means you need to get invoices out before the first of the month. About 30 days in advance is fine. We actually do ours ten days in advance. That's because everyone is on auto-pay so they only need an invoice for their records.

In my opinion, there is no reason you should not be paid in advance for any service that is fixed fee and monthly. You might be flexible about the date (1st, 2nd, 3rd of the month), but that's it. You are providing necessary and valuable services. You are committed to your suppliers for the month (e.g., anti-virus, spam filtering, RMM, PSA, email hosting). You have lots of legitimate reasons for being paid up front.

Exceptions to the policy: Okay, there are always exceptions, but you can standardize most of them. If clients absolutely refuse to pay with a credit card, you can let them pay by check. BUT it must arrive by the first of the month AND they need to pay three months at a time. I think we have four clients who took this route.

The other exception was my accountant. Helluva nice guy. Friend for 20+ years. We didn't make him sign up for managed services. We didn't make him pay in advance. But eventually we moved him onto one of our cloud plans ... and didn't give him an option. Everyone gets one "exception" client. :-)

Billing Policies for Project Labor

There are three easy ways to bill for project labor. And there are two types of project labor. The first type of project labor is "truly billable" labor that is not covered by managed services. For example, we cover the maintenance of the operating system and software. Adds, moves, and changes cost extra. So if we install a new program, that's billable.

The second type of project labor is actual projects such as migrations, installing a new equipment rack, or moving a client to a new MSP. This kind of labor might be flat-fee or hourly.

The first way to get paid for project labor is most relevant to flat-fee projects: Get X% up front and the remainder when the job is finished. Note that X can equal 100%.

The second way to get paid for project labor is via blocks of time. So, for example, the client pays you for ten hours of time and then they can chip away at it. When you would bill them an hour, you simply remove 1.0 hours from their credit on the books.

The third way to get paid for project labor is in arrears. That means that you bill the client after the work is done and they have a certain number of days to pay. Common time frames are 20 days and 30 days. I really wouldn't make it longer than that.

Because we have so little billable labor for clients on managed services, we bill in arrears for that. It's a very small amount and we have terms of net 20 days. Projects are billed at flat fee unless we really don't know what we're getting into. We ask for half up front and the rest upon completion. And that means ON completion - not 30 days later.

Billing Policies for Hardware and Software

This one is easy. We got into selling hardware and software when we didn't know anything about the business. We would run to the store and buy something, make very little profit, and then bill the client and let them pay in 30 days. Over time we started buying from real suppliers (e.g., Ingram and Synnex), making more profit, and much larger projects.

In other words, every part of our process evolved except payment.

Eventually, we adopted a very simple rule, and I believe you should do the same: We get paid in advance for all hardware and software orders.

This is easy to install. Write a memo and do it. "Beginning August 1st, all hardware and software purchases must be prepaid." That's it.

If clients would rather go online to Dell, HP, CDW, or Tiger Direct ... they will pay in advance with a credit card. Your clients pay in advance again and again and again with everyone else. You are simply coming up to speed with the 21st century.

There are two really great reasons to adopt this policy. First, you are never out of pocket for hardware and software purchases. That means you have conquered cash flow. Second, there are clients who give you the "go" and then change their mind. If the timing is wrong, you've ordered equipment and now you need to return it. In the meantime, you haven't been paid for it.

Life is much better when you get paid in advance for all hardware and software. Unlike monthly charges, we have never had any client argue about this or question it. Just do it.

Payment Policy Summary

Complete the following sentences:

Monthly recurring services will be billed ...

Project labor will be billed ...

Hardware and software will be billed ...

If you haven't reviewed your billing policies in some time (or ever), now is a great time to do it.

Three Take-Aways from This Chapter:

1. You should be paid in advance for as much as possible.
2. Adopt written policies on when you will bill clients for managed services, project labor, and hardware/software.
3. Draft one or more client memos and execute these policies!

Three Action Steps for Your Company:

1. ______________________________

____

2. ______________________________

____

3. ______________________________

____

18

Cash Flow: Getting Paid in Advance

Cash flow can kill your company - even if you're successful. When the money comes in after the bills are overdue, you have to scramble. Luckily, there are some simple strategies for staying ahead of the cash flow curve. In addition to making your life less stressful, positive cash flow will make your business more enjoyable and truly profitable.

This chapter is all about the most important rule of all: **Get Paid In Advance** as much as possible.

Overview

Unfortunately, many people start their small businesses with the assumption that they need to extend credit to their clients. A handful of entrepreneurs somehow escape this mindset and never fall prey to the cash flow trap. As a general rule for success, you should collect as much money as possible in advance.

Here's the basic problem: Timing.

And the basic reality: Money owed to you has a value less than one dollar per dollar.

The timing part is really the essence of cash flow. Let's say you do $10,000 worth of work. Due to different client arrangements and paying habits, you might expect:

$1,000 within the next week.

$3,000 more within the next two weeks.

$3,000 more within the next month.

$3,000 more within the next two months.

In reality, you have bills to pay next week, the week after, this month, and next month. Getting "paid" $10,000 is great. But your creditors don't care that you've extended credit to your customers. In this scenario, you'll pay your employees and your landlord more than once before you get your money.

And the sad truth is that old money has less value. Money that's more than 30, 60, 90 days old will probably be paid back with a "deal" that's less than face value. I've talked to many consultants who are owed $25,000 or $50,000. Some even more. Every one of these folks would happily take 75% of the total just to get the money now.

If you operate that way on an ongoing basis, then you need to build that into your rates. When you combine all clients, if you collect $90 for every $100 billed, then you need to adjust your budget to assume your effective billing rate is $90.

There are a handful of successful practices that can make all the difference with cash flow.

Start with the assumption that you'll get paid in advance whenever possible. To be honest, making this change during (or at the end of) a recession may be the best possible timing. You won't have to feel guilty about the change, and your clients will understand how tough things are.

Here are our basic "paid in advance" policies. See the previous chapter.

Hardware and Software must be paid in advance before you order it from the distributor. Period.

Project Labor must be paid in installments with a portion up front. The remainder should be paid on a schedule. The Schedule should be based on the completion of stages, not on a calendar schedule. If you give a calendar, make it an estimate and be clear that payments will be due upon the completion of stages.

All **Managed Service** payments are due on the first day of the month. If the client pays by credit card of debit card, the card is run on the first day of the month. If the client pays by check, she must pay for three months at a time, due on the 1st of the first month.

By ALL managed services, we include Hardware As A Service (HaaS), equipment rentals, remote monitoring and patch management, remote support, prepaid blocks of time, SPLA (Service Provider Licensing Agreement from Microsoft) or other licensing, and hosted services (spam filter, anti-virus, etc.). Anything that's billed regularly is paid in advance.

Cool. So now you're getting your money up front. In *Managed Services in a Month*, *Service Agreements for SMB Consultants*, and pretty much every other book on managed services, one of the greatest benefits you'll find is getting you money on the first day of the month.

There is a great joy in knowing that you've got the rent paid and all of the payroll covered. It really is a beautiful thing.

Timing is Everything

Let's look at two common examples of cash flow. First, here's what cash flow might look like if you have "terms" to be paid in arears.

Next we'll look at getting paid in advance. Note that the dollar amounts are the same.

Example One: Arears

Terms: Labor due net 30 days. Project labor net 30 days. Hardware net 20 days.

Rent due by the 5th.

Employees paid on the 10th and 25th of each month.

Table 18-1: Payment in Arears

Date	Action	Amount	Bank Balance
Sep. 30	Balance		$00.00
Oct. 1	Managed Service Billed	$5,000	$00.00
Oct. 2	Project Begins – Billed	$5,000	$00.00
Oct. 3	Rent Paid	-$1,500	-$1,500

Oct. 4	Hardware Billed	$2,000	-$1,500
Oct. 5	Hourly Labor Billed	$2,500	-$1,500
Oct. 10	Employee Paid	-$2,500	-$4,000
Oct. 10	Distributor Paid (HW)	-$1,800	-$5,800
Oct. 24	Hardware Paid	$2,000	-$3,800
Oct. 25	Employee Paid	-$2,500	-$6,300
Oct. 25	Hourly Labor Paid	$2,500	-$3,800
Oct. 30	Managed Service Paid	$5,000	$1,200
Oct. 30	Project Labor Paid	$5,000	$6,200

In the end, you had a good month. You made $6,200 (we're going to forget all of you other expenses for this example). But you were in the hole for MOST of the month – 22 days.

Where did that money come from? A line of credit loan? An investment from you, the owner? If you borrowed money, you need to pay it back with interest. And you don't get to get paid on payday with the rest of your employees.

Now let's see what it looks like when you get paid in advance.

Example Two Payment in Advance

Terms: Labor due in advance. Hardware due in advance.

Rent due by the 5th.

Employees paid on the 10th and 25th of each month.

Table 18-2: Payment in Advance

Date	Action	Amount	Bank Balance
Sep. 30	Balance		$00.00
Oct. 1	Managed Service Billed	$5,000	$5000
Oct. 2	Project Begins – Billed	$5,000	$10,000
Oct. 3	Rent Paid	-$1,500	$8,500
Oct. 4	Hardware Billed	$2,000	$10,500
Oct. 5	Hourly Labor Billed	$2,500	$13,000
Oct. 10	Employee Paid	-$2,500	$10,500
Oct. 10	Distributor Paid (HW)	-$1,800	$8,700
Oct. 25	Employee Paid	-$2,500	$6,200

Of course you see the difference. You spend ZERO days with a negative balance. You borrowed zero dollars from your line of credit.

You could even pay yourself $3,000 on the tenth of the month and still have plenty of money for everything. Then you could pay yourself another $3,000 on the twenty-fifth and still have money left over.

DO NOT think that this is just a made up example. This is real.

You can do this.

You should do this.

These re common, normal business practices and you should absolutely get paid in advance for (almost) everything you do. Any excuses you have for not doing this amount to fear.

Please calm your fears.

Do it. Do it. Do it.

Every single coaching client I've had will agree with me on this point: You will receive either zero client push-back or near-zero client push-back from these policies. They are simply and obvious.

And they can change your business.

Three Take-Aways from This Chapter:

1. Cash flow can kill your business. Get on top of it by getting paid in advance as much as possible.
2. Old money has less value. When people owe you money, they often pay it back at a discount.
3. Run real cash flow projections for your business – with options for payments in advance.

Three Action Steps for Your Company:

1. ______________________________

____

2. ______________________________

____

3. ______________________________

____

19

Collection Policies

The setup is this: You've either sold hardware/software or services and your client owes you money . . . but doesn't pay in a timely manner. See the last few chapters on getting paid in advance.

You can either have the client just pay you, or you can have them finance it through a leasing company. If they finance through a leasing company, you will normally get 100% of all products up front and 100% of labor within three days of the client signing off on completion of a project.

Notice that the leasing company gets a percentage of the total. They get paid for lending money and taking payments. That's a very strong clue that this behavior is worth paying extra for. In other words, it has value. So don't YOU give it to clients for free!

Anyway . . .

A client owes you money and they don't pay in a timely manner.

The key variables to consider are:

1) The amount in question

2) The paying habits of the client

3) The age of the debt

4) The contracts or ongoing agreements with the client

For example, we have a very simple rule about collections. On Monday, we review receivables. If any client has an outstanding balance greater than $500 that is past due, we assess a late fee of $25 and send them a note requesting payment. We also tell them that their account is "suspended." That means that we'll respond to emergencies, but we will not put updates to anti-virus, we will not monitor backups, etc. In other words, we won't provide them service until their bill is up to date.

Many clients have "learned" that Net 30 really means 30 days, but not really late until 30 days later, so they always pay on day 59. Whoever is teaching this stuff is really doing a disservice to their students.

You don't have to put up with it. First, set your terms to be Net 20. Then charge late fees on day 21. As a general rule, our first contact is something like this:

Dear Client:

Just a friendly reminder that the following invoice is overdue:

Inv. No.	*Inv. Date*	*Due Date*	*Inv. Amount*
12345	*02/03/2015*	*02/23/2013*	*$1,050.00*

If you have any questions about the amount you owe, please give us a call and we'll be happy to discuss it. If you've already sent your payment, please disregard this reminder.

We appreciate your continuing business, and we look forward to hearing from you shortly.

Sincerely,

Us

If you're not sure how to start a collection letter, go into QuickBooks and look at the same letters they've put together. QuickBooks has "friendly" and "harsh" letters. And of course you can Google collection letters to find more.

The important question is, what are your policies?

When a client invoices goes "late" what do you do? What's the first thing? What's the second thing? The easiest way to build this policy is with a timeline. For us this starts every Monday when we review past due invoices. If anyone owes more than $500, and it's past due, the office manager sends an email similar to the email above.

And she assesses a late fee.

On the first business day of the month, we assess a finance charge to all accounts that are overdue. QuickBooks has an automated feature for this.

If any accounts are 30 days past due, we cut off service, as described above.

In the very unusual event that someone is 60 days past due, we write them a letter cancelling the contract. (At a later date we can discuss the emotional "stuff" you feel about this. Suffice it to say for now that this is NOT your best client. And they don't respect you. And they don't love you.

No matter what other story you tell yourself in your head, you have a financial relationship with your clients. If they stop paying you, they break that relationship.

Please take note of Absolute Truth of Life #2: Money owed to you can never have a value of one dollar per dollar. In other words, you will collect less than the face value on ALL past due amounts. In most cases, you will settle for less. But in some cases, you will also pay an administrative assistant or a collection agency.

Old money is always collected at a discount. That's why it's critical to get paid in advance for as much as you can.

The sad truth is that we accept less than 100% of the money that's past due more than 30 days. So we end up giving a discount to the clients who pay late, while the client who pre-pay and pay on time are penalized.

What is your timeline? What's your process? Day 10, Day 20, Day 30, Day 60, etc.

Make this as automated as possible so that you don't get involved and extend the pain. Turn it over to your office staff and let the automated process take place.

Three Take-Aways from This Chapter:

1. Assess late fees on late payments.
2. Assess finance charges on past due amounts.
3. Turn over the collection process to someone who is not emotionally vesting in the relationship.

Three Action Steps for Your Company:

1. ______________________________

____

2. ______________________________

____

3. ______________________________

____

20

The Managed Services Grid

At several points in this book I refer to an Excel spreadsheet called the **Managed Services Grid.** Basically, this is a single spreadsheet you use to keep track of your clients and the services they are buying. It compliments your PSA and provides a cross-check.

There's no magic here. You probably have some variation of this. For us, the Managed Service Grid is one place where we keep track of all the numbers related to buying the components of managed service and selling managed services to our clients. There are basically two kinds of information here: Things we buy and things we sell.

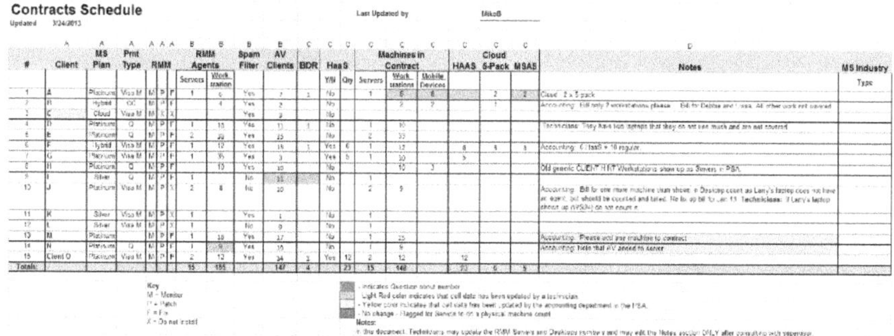

Contracts Schedule

Updated 3/24/2013 Last Updated by MikeB

#	Client	MS Plan	Prnt Type	RMM			RMM Agents		Spam Filter	AV Clients	BDR	HaaS		Machines in Contract			HAAS	Cloud 5-Pack	MSAS	Notes	MS Industry
							Servers	Workstation				Y/N	Qty	Servers	Workstations	Mobile Devices					Type
1	A	Platinum	Visa M	M	P	F	1	6	Yes	7	1	No		1	6	6		2	2	Cloud: 2 x 5 pack	
2	B	Hybrid	CC	M	P	F		4	Yes	2		No			2	2		1		Accounting: Bill only 2 workstations please. Bill for Debbie and Lissa. All other work not covered	
3	C	Cloud	Visa M	M	X	X			Yes	3		No									
4	D	Platinum	Q	M	P	F	1	10	Yes	11	1	No		1	10					Technicians: They have two laptops that they do not use much and are not covered	
5	E	Platinum	Q	M	P	F	2	30	Yes	25		No		2	33						
6	F	Hybrid	Visa M	M	P	F	1	12	Yes	18	1	Yes	6	1	12		6	[illegible]	[illegible]	Accounting: 6 HaaS + 10 regular.	
7	G	Platinum	Visa M	M	P	F	1	35	Yes	3		Yes	5	1	30		5				
8	H	Platinum	Q	M	P	F		10	Yes	10		No			10	3				Old generic CLIENT H KT Workstations show up as Servers in PSA.	
9	I	Silver	Q	M	P	F	1		No	31		No		1							
10	J	Platinum	Visa M	M	P	X	2	8	No	20		No		2	9					Accounting: Bill for one more machine than shown in Desktop count as Larry's laptop does not have an agent, but should be counted and billed. No lic up bill for Jan 13. Technicians: If Larry's laptop shows up (WS04) do not count it.	
11	K	Silver	Visa M	M	P	X	1		Yes	1		No		1							
12	L	Silver	Visa M	M	P	X	1		No	9		No		1							
13	M	Platinum		M	P	F	1	18	Yes	17		No		1	15					Accounting: Please add one machine to contract	
14	N	Platinum	Q	M	P	F	1	9	Yes	10		No		1	9					Accounting: Note that AV added to server	
15	Client O	Platinum	Visa M	M	P	F	2	12	Yes	34	1	Yes	12	2	12		12				
Totals:							15	155		147	4		23	15	148		23	6	5		

Key
M = Monitor
P = Patch
F = Fix
X = Do not install

- Indicates Question about number
- Light Red color indicates that cell data has been updated by a technician
- Yellow color indicates that cell data has been updated by the accounting department in the PSA
- No change - Flagged for Service to do a physical machine count

Notes:
In this document, Technicians may update the RMM Servers and Desktops numbers and may edit the Notes section ONLY after consulting with supervisor.

The Managed Services Grid

See the graphic here. When you register your book, you can download this in both PDF and Excel formats. See the "V1 Ch20 Managed Services Grid.xlsx" file.

Here's what you're looking at:

A. Client Info

Of course we track the client name. We also need to track how they pay, and the plans they have (such as Platinum Managed Services, Cloud services, and Hardware as a Service). Related to that, we track the nature of the monitoring we do. These include monitoring only, basic patching, fixes, or none of the above.

This information is found in the columns labeled Client, Payment Type, MS Plan, and RMM.

B. Services and Software We License

In terms of what we buy, we keep track of

- RMM (remote monitoring and management) agents

- Spam filter agents

- Anti-Virus agents

Each of these things is purchased by us on a per-unit basis. In some cases we sell them on the same basis. At other times we bundle them with other services. In all cases, we have to pay for every agent used that month - without regard to whether we got paid for it, sold it per each, or bundled it.

This information is found in the columns labeled RMM Agents, Spam Filter, and AV Clients.

C. The Services We Deliver To Each Client

In order to make sure the invoices are correct every month, you need to track the number of machines or devices under MS contract, cloud contract, HAAS, BDR, or some other service.

At some level, most of this exists in your PSA. But it's not all in one handy dandy spreadsheet. You need to coordinate this information between your bookkeeping/front office staff, your technical staff, and your PSA. The Managed Service Grid is more than just a cheat sheet for getting a quick glance of payment plans or the number of machines under contract.

It is also a tool you can use for communication within your company. Whether you use the system described here or another, you'll see how useful it can be. This spreadsheet can be used for asynchronous communication for your people. There are two basic rules for this communication.

1) You need a system for staff members to communicate clear, unambiguous information and questions. The following examples are based on the process we use.

a. If the front office manager has a question about any number in the table, she changes the background color to green and enters a note.

b. When a technician makes a change in the field, such as adding or removing a machine, he changes the appropriate cell to light red.

c. When the front office sees a light red cell, she makes the appropriate change in the PSA and then turns the cell to yellow.

d. When anyone has a question, they put notes in the notes field.

e. If, for whatever reason, you believe that the numbers in the real world are off from the contract numbers, then an on-site physical inventory is required. In such cases, the cell is colored red and a service request is created. The most common use for this is when you are on-boarding a new client.

f. Once the service manager has verified that the tech information has been entered into the contracts in the PSA, he sets the background color to "no background." This is the normal state unless a tech of the front office have a question. When notes have been addressed, they are cleared.

2) Everyone must absolutely and definitely use this system. You must be able to trust the system. That means that everyone uses it. Everyone must trust that everyone else has used the system and done their part.

This last point is critical. Like documentation itself, the process of maintaining the Managed Services grid is very easy and just takes a few minutes here or there. But if you get behind and can no longer trust it, then bringing it up to speed will take more time.

So, the Managed Service Grid is a tool you can use for communication. It is a way to verify how many agents (etc.) you are being billed for. It is a great way to track the services you should be billing. And it is a wonderful quick-reference guide for all of the above.

Keep It Up

The most common time that the MS Grid is used by a technician is when a machine is added to or removed from managed services. See the chapter in Volume Three of this series entitled "Adding a New Machine to Managed Services." Also see the last chapter in this volume, "Removing a Client from Managed Services."

The field tech's job is not to determine billing or discuss the contract with clients. His job is to make sure that machines added to or removed from service are reflected in the MS Grid.

The Service Manager will use the MS Grid much more frequently. For him, it's a reference tool. How many machines do they have? How many licenses are we buying? Etc.

Once a month, the Service Manager will verify that all the numbers on the grid are correct. If any cells are colored, he'll make sure that they are addressed. Then he'll verify that the billing numbers for contracts in the PSA are correct.

At the time of billing, the bookkeeper or office manager will once again verify that the MS Grid and PSA agree. Then she'll run the invoicing for the month. It's not her job to determine whether these numbers are correct, per se. It's only her job to verify that they agree with each other.

Once again, everyone who touches the document should do what they can to verify it is up to date and accurate.

You may from time to time add or remove information from the MS Grid. I *highly* recommend that you always use a copy. Even copy the worksheet and rename it as an old version. Then you can make changes to the new version and you'll have an "in place" archive of the old format.

Obviously, the overall format won't change once you are tracking everything you need to in the MS Grid.

Three Take-Aways from This Chapter:

1. A single Excel worksheet is a good place to keep a snapshot of your clients, what you buy, and what you sell.
2. Create a system that allows each user of the MS Grid to provide changes and asynchronous communication.
3. Make using the grid a regular habit for everyone.

Three Action Steps for Your Company:

1. ______________________________

____

2. ______________________________

____

3. ______________________________

____

21

Invoice Review and Processing

As strange as it sounds, there's a simple habit that separates companies with good cash flow and companies without: Good Billing Practices. That means sending out accurate invoices, sending them out in a timely manner, and enforcing reasonable payment terms. We've already discussed payment terms.

There are two processes detailed here since the function of reviewing time entries is typically done by the service manager while expenses and products are reviewed by the office manager or accountant. Once you get this ironed out, it should go very quickly. This is particularly true if your services are structured so that most labor is included in managed services.

I recommend doing your billing once a week. If you take care of this every Monday, it will be super-quick and you'll never be out of touch with your accounts receivable. One of my rules for life is that you get better at whatever you put your attention on. Put attention on your finances, and you'll improve your finances.

A Few Notes About The Process

1. Always work from the top of the list to the bottom systematically

2. Check the Company off only when the review of individual Time entries is complete

3. It is suggested that you open a second instance of the PSA system to do research or make changes. You can flip between the two instances with a simple alt-tab. (Note that some changes will not show correctly until the search is re-run.)

4. Be consistent in annotating the Notes sections of the time entries. Keep Credit notes one line below tech notes. There is a list of commonly used notes at the end of this chapter.

5. Remember that any system covered under Managed Services must have notes supporting why we *should* bill for a given time entry and systems not covered must have notes supporting why we *should not* bill them for a given time entry.

6. All steps in this process are necessary and are in a particular order. None should be skipped even if you believe you know the process.

Obviously, you will need to adjust the process to fit your PSA system.

Process One (for the tech manager): Reviewing Invoice Time Entries

1. Log into the PSA system and navigate to the Invoice Wizard

2. Set the "Through Date" to reflect the most recent Saturday or end of desired billing cycle.*

* When billing weekly, we recommend a billing period that starts on Sunday and ends on Saturday. In addition to being a standard week, this gives you time to settle all work and time entries for the previous week before you do billing on Monday.

3. Sort the list from greatest Bill Amount to least. You will work through the companies from those with the most work to those with the least.

4. Select the first Company in the list to review the Time entries

5. Start by clearing all the checkboxes for Time entries. They must be reviewed before they can be considered accepted and the checkboxes will be what keeps track of your progress.

6. For each company, sort so the oldest entries are at the bottom of the list and newest at the top. Start with the oldest entries first. This is because billing of previous items can effect decisions for billing of newer items.

7. Verify that the Agreement (contract) field is cleared or set to the correct agreement based on the client and the system being worked on. Note: This may be changed later for items that are initially believed to be covered under managed services but will be billed for some reason.

8. If an item is completed but not "closed," change the status to Closed.

9. Verify the Work Type field is correct. Change as needed. This is critical as the minimum hours billable depends on the Work Type.

10. Verify the Billable field is correct. By default all work is Billable, all travel is "No Charge," and we never use "Do Not Bill."

11. Review the Time entry for Onsite and Remote Minimums.

a. For Regular Onsite and After Hours:

- If the Actual Hours is less than 1 hour, determine if there were any other time entries for the same technician on the same visit.
- If there are other time entries for the same visit, adjust the Invoice Hours field to match the Actual Hours field.
- Double check that the total Invoice Hours of all time entries during the visit add up to the onsite minimum. If it does not, adjust the last entry to bring the total up to the minimum.

b. For Regular Remote:

- If the Actual Hours is less than 0.5 hours, determine if there were any other time entries for the same technician during the remote session.
- If there are other time entries for the same session, adjust the Invoice Hours field to match the Actual Hours field.
- Double check that the total Invoice Hours of all time entries during the session add up to the remote minimum. If it does not, adjust the last entry to bring the total up to the minimum.

12. Review the main Notes section for content and clarity and to ensure it always ends with "Documented work." Edit as needed.

13. Review the Actual hours field for this time entry. If it exceeds what is a reasonable time for the task:

   a. Adjust the Invoice Hours accordingly. Note: If all time will be credited, simply change the Billable field to No Charge.

b. Enter a note at the end of the main Notes section for the client to see.

Note: Time entries that are longer than reasonable for the task must be carefully evaluated. It is most likely that the tech did not enter sufficient notes to support the time on site or the tech was in training on the task. If a little clarification from the tech can validate the billing and it is worth the time, contact the tech. Either way, the tech must be reminded of the process and encouraged to have excellent notes from the start.

14. Review Internal Notes and revise entries as follows:

a. Items marked as "Time logged against SR xxxx"

- Adjust the Invoice Hours to reflect 0 (we don't charge for internal notes).
- Enter a note at the end of the main Notes section for the client to see.

b. Items marked as "Credit Client . . ."

- Review the reason given by the tech and adjust the Invoice Hours accordingly. Note: If all time will be credited simply change the Billable field to No Charge.
- Enter a note at the end of the main Notes section for the client to see.

c. Items marked as either Not covered or Billable.

- Review the reason given by the tech and if any of the time will be billed, change the Agreement field to the "Billable Time and Materials" Agreement and adjust the Invoice Hours accordingly.
- Enter a note at the end of the main Notes section for the client to see.

15. Verify that there are not a number of duplicate notes. Basically, clean up the time entry so that is will be as easy to use in the future if you need to look at it and all people involved have forgotten the details.

16. Save and close the entry. Check the box for that item and go on to the next.

17. When all Time entries have been reviewed for a specific company, return to the search list and check the box for that company and go on to the next.

18. Repeat the above process until all bills for all companies have been reviewed.

19. Compose and send an email to the bookkeeper informing them that Invoice Review is complete and indicating any issues or reservations with any of the entries.

Process Two: Bookkeeper Review of Invoice Expense and Product Entries

1. Log into the PSA system and run the Invoice Wizard

2. Change the "Through Date" to reflect the most recent Saturday or end of desired billing cycle

3. Select the first Company in the list to review the Expense and Product entries

4. Verify that our expenses are not reflected on the client invoice

5. Generate an invoice for all products. Note: We invoice products separately in case there are disputes about labor. We do not want to wait for payment on products simply because they were included on an invoice with labor.

6. Make sure invoices in the PSA and in QuickBooks are in synch. You might do this manually if you have low volume, or use the connection tool built into the PSA system.

Note: Invoices are generated in PDF format and mailed to the client contact.

Terms To Use When Annotating "Free" Time Entries

Always start the annotation with "Note: Credited x.x hour(s)" - " i.e. Note: Credited 0.5 hours – Time in excess of quoted."

Here are some sample phrases to use:

- "All hours covered under Managed Services Agreement"
- "Time logged against another Service Request"
- "Time in excess of reasonable"
- "Time in excess of reasonable for the project (or task)"
- "Time in excess of quote"
- "Duplicate work performed"
- "No billable work performed"
- "KPE Research"
- "No charge per ____________ [tech/manager]

Three Take-Aways from This Chapter:

1. Create checklists for ticket billing review (service managers) and invoicing (bookkeeper).
2. Verify that your policies are clear and documented with regard to what's billable, when you give away non-billable labor, etc.
3. The service manager and bookkeeper should communicate extensively about this process until they always agree on what is billable and when to bill it.

Three Action Steps for Your Company:

1. ______________________________

____

2. ______________________________

____

3. ______________________________

____

22

Cash Flow Weekly Procedure

Cash flow can make or kill your business. Even if you're technically "profitable," you can run out of money to pay your bills. It's largely a matter of timing. See the earlier discussions about terms and payments in Chapters 17-19.

For example, if you are owed $10,000 for work you've done, then you have a $10,000 "asset" called accounts receivable. But if that money won't come in for 30-45 days, it really does you no good. So, if you have $8,000 in bills due during that period, you have to come up with the money somehow. If you borrow and spend $8,000, then you have to be very disciplined to pay all that back when the $10,000 rolls in.

Think of money flowing INTO and OUT OF your business in 30, 60, and 90 day intervals. Balancing income and outgo can be difficult, especially since unexpected expenses always seem to arise.

With luck, you are making good progress on getting paid in advance. If you need help implementing such a policy, I can help you make it happen in short order. I will write up the policy, announce it to your clients, collect credit card information, and set up all the automatic payments. I charge $250/hour for that service (paid in advance), so you might want to consider doing it yourself. It's really easy.

So anyway . . .

Now we need to monitor our cash as it flows into and out of the company.

I am a firm believer that the business owner needs to have a SIMPLE way to keep an eye on cash flow in order to make good decisions. For me, this means looking at basic cash flow numbers at least once a week. And to make the process even more relevant to daily operations, I think it's good to look at cash flow in relation to the largest expense you have: Payroll.

Quite simply, how are you doing with regard to money in the bank between now and the next two pay days? I choose two pay days because we pay twice a month (on the 10th and 25th). But our managed service contracts are all paid on the first of the month.

Note: Most clients pay us on a monthly basis. This is prepaid by credit card. Cards are run automatically on the first of the month. Depending on the card processor, the money settles into our account and is usable three business days later. Given weekends and Monday holidays, this means that the money might not be available to us for as much as six calendar days.

If clients choose to pay by check, they must pay for three months at a time. We call these "quarterlies" even though the quarter can start any month. Ideally, quarterlies are staggered so we don't have huge peaks and valleys.

The other key variable to consider is Accounts Payable - money we have to spend. We use QuickBooks to enter bills as they arrive. So we can look at AP and know what needs to be spent between now and the next pay period. See the table below. These are just fictional numbers to illustrate.

This spreadsheet is included with the downloadable material for this book.

	A	B	C	D	E
1		**Cash Flow Report**		**Updated:**	**August 31, 2014**
2					
3				Amount	Running Total
4	Cash On Hand - Bank Checking			$2,570	$2,570
5					
6	A / R Hourly Labor by	9/10/2014	+	$5,000	$7,570
7	A/R from Managed Svc			$20,000	$27,570
8	A/R from HW / SW			$4,000	$31,570
9	A/P by	9/10/2014		$9,200	$22,370
10	**Payroll due**	**9/10/2014**	-	**$11,500**	$10,870
11					
12	A / R Hourly Labor by	9/25/2014	+	$3,500	$14,370
13	A/R from Managed Svc			$2,500	$16,870
14	A/R from HW / SW			$4,000	$20,870
15	A/P by	9/25/2014		$8,500	$12,370
16	**Payroll due**	**9/25/2014**	-	$11,500	$870
17					
18					
19					
20	Note: Based on paying employees on the 10th and 25th of each month.				

This Excel spreadsheet is NOT a super-detailed view of finances. It is a simple overview of the most basic information we need. Here's what you see there:

Date.

This spreadsheet was run at the end of November. So it's after the last pay period for the month and before the first pay period for the next month.

Cash on Hand.

This is literally the bottom line in the QuickBooks check register we use for paying all operational expenses, including payroll.

Accounts Receivable.

We only list money here that we are sure will come in. So, if a client just received a bill and might not pay in the next few days, we don't count that. But if someone has terms of net 20 (our default), and an invoice has been out for ten days, then we are sure the money will come in.

We list quarterly payments that will be received. Again, these are checks that pay for three months service. Because the three months can start any time, this number varies from month to month.

Finally, we list monthly payments. These are clients who pay by credit card. This money "just shows up" on the first of the month. This number only changes if we add or lose a client, or if the number of machines on managed service changes. These numbers are based on contract amounts in our PSA system.

Accounts Payable.

These are the bills we expect to pay between now and the next payroll date (the 10th). This number is larger during the first part of the month than the second because many bills roll in around the first and are due shortly thereafter (e.g., rent).

Payroll Due.

This is an estimate based on previous payrolls and the estimated hours we expect to pay.

Rinse, Repeat.

Notice that we also estimate income and outgo for the next pay period (the 25th).

Benefits

As simple as it sounds, you need to know whether you'll have an easy time or a tough time making payroll. Should you put off paying a bill? Should you restrict hours or give a tech the day off to save money? More importantly, how are you doing with the NEXT payroll? If you charge all the credit cards on the first of the month, the first payroll is easy. But if you have too much break/fix labor and not enough managed services, the second payroll might be difficult.

The primary benefit of this procedure is to have peace of mind. You can plan two or four weeks in advance.

But right away you'll find yourself thinking a little more strategically. Do you really need this or that? Should the tech hours be expanded or contracted? Will you be able to take an extra owner's draw this month?

With this process in place, you will also be able to see cash accumulate as you prepare for an upcoming annual payment (e.g., worker's comp insurance, or annual Microsoft dues).

As you tune into your cash flow you will get a real sense of how money actually "flows" into and out of your company. Remember: you get better at whatever you put your attention on. So if you want to get better at finances, paying attention to cash flow is a great place to start. Look at this Excel spreadsheet at least once a week!

I am amazed at how many people have been in business for five or ten years and cannot rattle off their monthly or weekly cash flow numbers. As you work with this information, it will become an important piece of your decision making process. If a program costs

$250/month, what will that do to your cash flow? If you hire a new technician, how many hours can he work?

And at a more basic level, are income and expenses in line with one another? Is one growing faster than the other? Is there a trend, or was that a one-time event?

Implementation Notes

Implementing this process is easy.

First, create a spreadsheet like the one pictured above. It's not too hard to figure out.

Second, for each pay period, copy the worksheet and create a new one. Name them based on pay period (e.g, Jan 10, Jan 25, Feb 10).

Third, go through this at least once a week. Monday is probably best. If you have an office manager, go through it with her. She should be able to fill in most or all of these numbers.

Fourth, once you determine that you have X dollars to spend on paying invoices, go ahead and mark them to be paid in QuickBooks. As soon as you're done reviewing cash flow, have your office manager print out the checks for the invoices you decided to pay.

Interestingly enough, that last little habit might tempt you to look at cash flow again tomorrow. Don't worry. That's a good thing.

One of the keys to success here is to Keep It Simple! Don't junk up the cash flow spreadsheet with details about types of expenses or detailed dates. The more complicated it is, the less likely you are to execute the process regularly!

This entire process takes no more than 15 minutes. So it helps you run your business better, but it's not difficult or time consuming.

Benefits

The greatest benefit of watching cash flow is that you will become more profitable. How? Well, you'll plan a little more and probably spend a little less. You'll borrow less money and pay fewer penalties.

The more you take time to step back from executing your business and spend time examining it, the better your business will become. You will find yourself thinking more strategically about how you handle and manage money.

Holding a Mirror Against Your Warts

Warning. Some of this might not be fun. Within the first one or two weeks, this process will reveal whether you have huge problems with your business finances. The huge (potential) problems are 1) No regular income, and 2) Accounts receivable that's out of control.

When you start out with this procedure, you might find that your numbers are irregular or unpredictable. If so, that means that your A/R for hourly labor (break/fix) is too high. If you can't plan two weeks in advance to know what you're going to receive, then you have little or no managed service revenue. I'm not kidding you when I say that I would not have ANY employees unless I could point to a spreadsheet that showed how I'm going to pay them in the next two weeks.

With break/fix labor, the stream of money coming in can be very unpredictable. You will see this painfully clear as soon as you look at your numbers. If nothing else has motivated you to sign some service agreements, look at cash flow! We want to guarantee that we can cover our monthly expenses based on guaranteed revenue on the first day of the month!

As you monitor cash flow, you will see this monthly (and quarterly) number go up and up over time. As that number goes up, your stress will go down.

The other huge problem is accounts receivable. You shouldn't have any! Or at least you shouldn't have much. If all hardware and software is pre-paid (see Chapter Eighteen) and managed services are paid on the first of the month, then the only accounts receivable you have is for incidental hourly jobs and projects.

Projects are great. We always get paid in advance for the core of a project. That means 90% of the money up front and the rest is the "expected but unpredictable" piece of fine-tuning a project.

If you've read my blogs or books, then you know that I am **adamantly opposed** to giving credit for 30, 60, or 90 days. I hear all kinds of excuses about why that's not possible because your clients are different from every other client on earth. Well they're not. They're just not. You know that big corporation that says they never pay in advance? They do. They just don't pay YOU in advance. That government agency? Same thing.

The most successful consulting companies all get paid in advance. The ones who won't stand up to big money and demand it get paid in 30, 60, 90, or whenever.

If you have accounts receivable, you will be paid less than 100% of what's owed. Period.

This is an absolute truth of business. You might get 75% or 85% or even 90%. But you will never be paid 100% of the money you are owed when you extend credit.

You can believe me or you can learn from experience. Most people who learn from experience assume that their hard earned lesson was a one-time deal with a crappy client that they'll never have to worry about again. But believe me, there are plenty of other people willing to take your services and pay you less than fair value. Ignore the lesson or learn the lesson: the choice is yours.

As you look at your cash flow on a weekly basis, you will become acutely aware of the difference between **money you are owed** and **money you will be paid**. Note that "money you are owed" is NOT on the Excel spreadsheet. Why? Because it doesn't matter. The money you are owed is irrelevant. It is unimportant. It is FICTION.

The reality is that you have to focus very closely on a much smaller number: "Accounts Receivable For Sure." That's reality. That's the money you KNOW you're going to receive. Someone owes you $30,000 or $10,000? All of your clients combined owe you $15,000? So what? You can't spend that. You can't use it for payroll. You can't take it to the bank. You can't do anything with it.

The only money that matters is the money you are actually going to receive in the next 10-15 days. Actually. Really.

Why? Because you can actually spend money that you receive. You can pay employees with real money. You can pay rent with real money. Promised money that might show up is not relevant to running your business. As you go through your cash flow week after week, focusing only on the "Accounts Receivable For Sure," you will begin to realize that you need to beat down and eliminate your accounts receivable.

Banks and accountants think accounts receivable are an *asset* to your business. But if you're a small business, they are a cancer that can eat you alive. Eliminate accounts receivable until you have revenues over $2 million/year. Then keep AR as small as possible.

Three Take-Aways from This Chapter:

1. You should have an accurate estimate of your cash flow at least once per week.
2. It is very important that you get good at estimating how much money you can absolutely count on in the next week.
3. Managing cash flow is one of the most important elements of your long term financial success.

Three Action Steps for Your Company:

1. ____________________

   ____

2. ____________________

   ____

3. ____________________

   ____

23

Hourly vs. Salaried Employees

When you have employees, one of the most important questions you need to address is how you pay them. The two most common options are to pay hourly and to pay a flat fee per month (salary).

This is also a very highly regulated element of business, so the simple division between hourly and salary isn't that simple any more. Many states have adjusted the "rules" about these two types of employment, applying a variety of requirements and options that might surprise you.

Here are some thoughts on developing a policy that works for you.

Salary

Salary employment means that you agree to pay based on an annual sum, divided evenly by the number of pay periods in the year. For example, a salary of $60,000 and a monthly payroll would result in twelve payments of $5,000 each. Minus taxes, deductions, etc.

Normally, salaries are reserved for supervisors, executives, and managers. Others may be eligible in your state. There are both Federal and State laws about this. In most cases, salaried employees keep track of their time, but only so the employer can calculate things like the cost of delivering services. An employee's salary is stable whether they work 30 hours or 60. (There are some exceptions to this in some states.)

The primary benefit that most employers see is that they can **work their employees harder** without paying more money. So lunch times disappear and employees are encouraged to stay late, come in on weekends, and not receive extra money. The employer has a stable cost and can (theoretically) increase profit by getting additional "free" labor out of the employee.

In reality, salaried employees tend to receive higher benefits, take off more time during the work day for (paid) trips to the bank and for medical appointments. In other words, the employees make up for a lot of that extra work by taking time where they can find it.

And, to be honest, a good employer won't take advantage of employees.

Hourly

Hourly employees are just that: Paid per hours worked. The norm is that you have to pay extra for overtime, normally 1.5 times the standard rate. You can pay more. In some jurisdictions, the 1.5x number is required by law. In California, overtime is calculated every day as well as every week. So anything over 8 hours is overtime, even if the employee is not over 40 hours for the week.

Many hourly employees are not paid benefits. But we offer the same benefits to anyone who regularly works 30 or more hours per week. Benefits can be very expensive or very manageable, so you need to consider them carefully (we'll cover benefits in Volume Two of this series).

The great advantage for employers offering hourly labor is that you can increase and decrease the hours as needed to stay profitable. This is sometimes tough on employees, but not always. We have been amazed, especially with young employees, that they don't want 40 hours a week. Some of them are constantly taking a day here and a day there just to go fishing. Many like leaving at 4:00 PM.

We had one employee for three years who almost NEVER worked more than 37 hours a week, no matter how much work there was to do. And it's not because we pay too much.

[Side note: Money is NOT much of a motivator for employees. I know that sounds odd as a manager/owner. But most employees are looking for other ways to be satisfied in their jobs. There are seven million articles on this.

Here's one: “Is Money an Effective Motivator at Work?” by Taras Bereza. Also, please read *Drive* by Daniel Pink – all about what motivates people.]

You can also have additional pay levels. For example, you can pay 2x for work after 12 hours in a day or for work on holidays. Just don't make it too complicated.

Super Important Advice:

If you CAN pay hourly, you have a huge tool for managing your expenses when workflow diminishes.

Employee expenses are the single greatest expense you have. When you have a cash flow crunch, cutting employee expenses is sometimes the only meaningful way to reduce your overhead.

It is hard to lay people off or reduce hours. But your business' survival may depend on it. Paying employees by the hour allows you to reduce hours and see a pretty quick cash flow change. With salaried employees, they're either ON or OFF the payroll, which can be tough.

If you can, I recommend that you pay your employees by the hour.

Bonuses

There are many ways to set bonuses and many kinds of bonuses to offer. We could have a whole separate chapter on this. But the most important thing to remember is:

Only pay bonuses from net profits . . . and only if you're exceeding your established goals.

Ooooops. You don't have established goals for profitability? Well, take care of that!

Holidays

One big difference between salaried and hourly employees is how holidays are handled. If someone is on salary, they are not generally required to work holidays. Your company needs to post an official list of your company holidays. Post it for employees - and tell your clients.

If you don't do this, you'll have people saying "It's Groundhog Day. Everyone knows that."

There are Federal Holidays and State Holidays. You might add the employee's birthday as a holiday. You might add the day after Thanksgiving (as we do), or choose not to celebrate Columbus Day (we don't).

Like everything else: It doesn't really matter what you do here, as long as you have an agreed upon policy and you post it.

Hourly employees are another story. Generally speaking, if they're not scheduled to work on holidays, then they don't get paid for holidays. If they are scheduled, however, then you might want to pay more for working the holidays. You are not required to do this, so you need to decide what your policy is.

Posters and Advice

As you can see, this topic can be quite overwhelming.

Each state, plus the Federal government, have posters with many of the most important rules and regulations. You need to post these somewhere. In California they take up approximately one entire wall of the break room.

Believe it or not, those posters can be a great guide to what you can do, what you have to do, and what you can't do. There are a few that actually have blank spots for you to fill in variables like rate of pay for overtime.

Good advice can also be found with your payroll service. We have used ADP, Paychex, small Mom-and-Pop payroll services, and those offered through the bank. In all cases there was someone who knows a LOT about employment rules and regulations. You're paying for this with your monthly fees, so you might as well use it.

Another good source of advice is your accountant or enrolled agent. They may offer a payroll service. But if nothing else, they will know someone. Get a referral to a specialist.

I'm not a big fan of downloading someone else's sample employee handbook from the Internet unless you intend to pay your attorney to vet it for your state/province. But there are good, reasonably-priced, up-to-date sample handbooks for sale for every state and province. As I mentioned before, this is a very highly regulated area, so don't put yourself in a position to do things illegally because you got the wrong sample.

We have an employee handbook based 95% on a product sold by the California Chamber of Commerce. All changes have been approved by our attorney. We have a lawyer that we use to advise us on all employment matters. We don't give him a lot of work, but enough that he knows who we are when we call.

An employee handbook is different from a company handbook or company policy book. An employee handbook only deals with the policies around employee and “rules” you have about employment within the company. This might include how to schedule time off, for example. But it would not cover the procedure for on-site client visits. That kind of thing has to do with how your company operates and promotes your brand.

Final Notes

If you do what makes sense and seems like the right thing to do, you'll probably be just fine. If you use a big payroll service like ADP or Paychex, their processes will help keep you within the law.

But take this stuff very seriously and develop processes and written procedures so you don't have to just make stuff up when an issue comes up.

And please consider paying hourly if you can. It might save your business when cash flow gets tight.

Three Take-Aways from This Chapter:

1. Payroll is the single largest expense in your company. You should have policies to address it.
2. If it's possible to pay hourly, doing so will give you much great control over the largest expense in your company.
3. Find a sample employee handbook – one that's written for your state or province.

Three Action Steps for Your Company:

1. ____

   ____

2. ____

   ____

3. ____

   ____

24

Running Regular Financial Reports

It always strikes me as odd that business owners hate dealing with money. I know, we didn't get into business to count pennies, balance QuickBooks, and mess with the messy side of finances. But this is not a hobby. We did go into business. And businesses exist to make money for their owners.

I've written several articles about finances, especially some year-end commentaries. These are included in the downloadable content when you register this book. Just look for the "End of Year Finances" articles.

This chapter is about the Financial Reports you should be running on a regular basis. "Regular" does not mean every report needs to be run every month. There are weekly reports, monthly reports, quarterly reports, and annual reports.

Setting Up QuickBooks

As you know, you need to set up QuickBooks with the correct categories so that you can track money. Your details will be different from my details. But however you set up your categories, you need to keep track of three primary elements: **Income, Expenses, and Profit**. For our purposes, income and revenue are interchangeable.

Never, ever, ever confuse revenue with profit. The math is:

Revenue - Expenses = Profit

Everyone wants to brag about the client that pays them $10,000 a month. I'll take a buncha those. But no one brags about the client who costs $9,500 a month to support. Here's why.

Let's say client #1 brings in revenue of $1,000 a month and costs $500 to support. Profit = $500.

Let's say client #2 brings in revenue of $10,000 a month and costs $9,500 to support. Profit = $500.

Which client would you rather have? Client #1 - because they're a LOT easier to support. That "big" client is a pain in the butt. I know that because they used to be my client. I fired them because they were taking all the administrative time in our company and producing the majority of stress in my brother's life.

How do you know whether a client is profitable (and how profitable)? Well, you need to set up your QuickBooks properly. Then you need to use it religiously. You need a good PSA system, and you need to use it religiously.

One of the key things we had to work out with both ConnectWise and Autotask is the **accurate** tracking of time spent on a client. This includes all the unbillable or "covered" time that's included in managed service agreements and projects. We like to run flat-fee projects. It is critically important to keep track of time so that we know whether a project (or a month of managed service) is profitable or not.

I have covered this extensively in the book *Project Management in Small Business* (with Dana Goulston, PMP) and in various articles and audio programs.

If you spend 40 hours on a project that brings in $5,000, are you profitable? How do you know? What do you track? What's your real cost? Between QuickBooks and your PSA, you should be able to figure this out.

Weekly Reports

Your only real immediate need for information has to do with **cash flow**. Can you pay the bills coming up? In Chapter Twenty-Two we discussed your Cash Flow Weekly Procedure. Basically, you need to track all the money that's coming in and going out so that you know what needs to happen between now and the next payday, or between now and the end of the month. Keeping track of finances in real-time will give you great clarity on what you should be doing with your time.

Another weekly report you should run is **employee utilization**. It's not as critically important as cash flow, but employee utilization reports provide you with some very important variables you need to track profitability – and to make accurate estimates for future profitable projects.

Employee utilization reports tell you how much money you're making on each technician. To do this, you need to have your PSA set up properly . . . and you need to be using it.

Employees need to keep accurate track of their time. That means they need to be working in real time. When that happens, you can accurately track time spent on administrative tasks, managed service labor, and truly billable labor.

For small shops, don't be surprised at all if your technicians are about 50% billable. That sounds low, but there are all kinds of reasons for it, especially if you don't bill for travel time. When technicians drive all over the county doing small jobs, the billable percentage goes down. When they sit at their desk doing remote support, billability goes up.

Let's say you have a tech who is paid 40 hours a week. You have one big service meeting and two little ones in a week. That's two hours. He spends an hour each day checking email (4 x 15 minutes). That's another five. If it takes 20 minutes to drive to the average client and he visits two clients a day, that's 400 minutes a week or about 6.5 hours. And, because you're a nice boss, you pay him for half an hour a day to study for a Microsoft or Cisco exam. That's another 2.5 hours. Total non-billable time is 16 hours.

24 billable hours divided by 40 hours = 60% billable.

(Note: That "billable" time might be covered by managed services. Don't confuse yourself around this. You are being paid for it. You need to track it as billable time to differentiate it from truly not-billable time.)

How do you use this number? We'll discuss that in Volume Three of this series of books. But here's a quick example. Let's say a project takes 60 hours. Your tech is 60% billable. Therefore, you need to pay your technician for 100 hours in order to have 60 available to sell on the project.

Monthly Reports

In the "End of Year Finances - Pt 2" article referenced above, I talk about some of the monthly reports you need to generate. These include:

1. Largest Months. This is a list of the largest sales months in your business history. I produce a list of the twelve largest months. Ideally, these will be the twelve most recent months, but that's just not the case. If the month just finished is on the twelve largest ever, then you have an update to this report. Otherwise, no update.

2. Most Profitable Months. Remember, the largest sales months are not the same as the most profitable months. Ideally, they will be, but that's not the reality of the business world. This report is interesting because it keeps your analytical mind aware of the fact that revenue and profit are not the same. When your emotional mind gets excited about a large sale, your analytical mind will step in and inquire about profitability.

3. The Largest Clients. You might report this for the previous twelve months, three months, or one month. In fact, you could substitute "Most Profitable Clients" for largest clients. The report you choose to generate is not as important as the fact that you generate it. You and your employees should know where the money comes from.

Sometimes, loud and troublesome clients are not the largest, or the most profitable. Don't leave a $5,000/month managed service client hanging because a break/fix pain-in-the-butt client is making a lot of noise.

There are many other reports you can generate, but don't get too fancy unless your business is large enough to actually get value from the reports. This might include

- The total number of service requests opened and closed in the previous month
- A breakdown of Priority 1, 2, 3, and 4 service requests in the previous month
- Clients with the most SRs in the previous month
- Clients who consumed the most hours in the previous month
- Average time to close a P1 service request (and P2, P3, P4) in the previous month
- Earnings per employee

- Sales per sales person
- EBITDA % (earnings before interest, taxes, depreciation, and amortization)

Quarterly Reports

You can do a number of these reports on a quarterly basis, whether calendar quarters or a rolling 3-month report.

But the most important quarterly report you can generate is a simple 1-2 page "Quarterly Report" to deliver to your company at a meeting. This report is more of a narrative to let them know how you're doing, what's working, the challenges you face, and where you want to go in the quarter ahead. Here's the kind of thing you might include:

- Overview. For each of the major goals for the quarter, how did you do? Report on employees hired and departed.
- Profitability. Are sales up, down, or even? Are they on target? Is profit up, down, or even. Is it on target?
- Major goals for the new Quarter.
- A reminder or two about the vision and mission of your company. Tie these into the quarterly goals and activities.
- If you have written 1-year and 5-year goals, how are you progressing? How will the actions of the next quarter affect that?

Annual Reports

Annual reports are another thing. There's an old maxim that you have to start acting like the company you want to be. I've seen clients who will never be publicly traded, but they acted as if they were because they wanted to grow their companies significantly, and big companies make annual reports to their shareholders.

An annual report is a combination of all of these. It presents the finances with a little deeper analysis. It also presents a discussion of the goals and vision/mission with a deeper analysis. You might not write out your annual report for your employees, but you should absolutely go over it with all stockholders (including your spouse) and managers.

The end of the year/beginning of the New Year is an "obvious" time to get started on these reports. But there's never a bad time.

Of course I recommend a binder with tabs. Once you have someone to help with your finances, you can just show them how to run the reports you want and put them in the binder for you. That way all you have to do is review the information.

Sole Proprietor? To be honest, generating all these reports yourself is a GREAT exercise in understanding how money flows in, through, and out of your company.

As always, you need to find a system that works for you. But you should put significant emphasis on the financial side of your business. Remember two key lessons.

First,

"You will get better at whatever you put your attention on." (Palachuk)

And Second,

"What gets measured gets done." (Peter Drucker)

Three Take-Aways from This Chapter:

1. Running regular financial reports will keep your finger on the pulse of your business.
2. You can't just run reports from your PSA or QuickBooks: Some have to be more hand-crafted.
3. Once you've documented how to get the reports you need, pass that chore onto someone else.

Three Action Steps for Your Company:

1. ______________________________

   ____

2. ______________________________

   ____

3. ______________________________

   ____

25

Choosing Pay Dates

When you start to have employees, your business changes in many ways. Sometimes the simplest decisions have dramatic impacts on your operations and finances. A great example of that is the choice of pay dates.

The decision about when to set pay dates affects cash flow more than anything else. But it also has a significant effect on staff morale and their cash flow. So, without regard to the bank or the payroll process per se, I'm going to talk about the effect of payroll dates on **cash flow** and **employees**.

Because payroll is the biggest piece of your budget, it is also the biggest element in your cash flow calculation. You would think that pay dates would be a very simple thing, given the fact that every business with employees has figured it out. But there are some gotchas you have to avoid.

The biggest lesson we had to learn was the **frequency of paydates**. Your state or province has requirements regarding this matter. Google "pay date regulations " to start researching. Of course, the official governing agency in your state is the final word on this.

In California, no employer can pay monthly except the State of California. Everyone else must pay at least twice a month. That means, generally:

- Every two weeks
- At two set times for the month

or

- Weekly

Paying weekly is great for cash flow, generally, because you need less money for each payroll period. But it increases the "hassle" level because it seems like you're always processing payroll. Whether you do it in-house or pay someone, you'll need to make sure time cards are all in and settled before payroll rolls around again. It also means you need to maintain a steady level of cash in your account at all times.

Weekly pay can also be a hassle for employees that are not good at setting aside a little each week toward rent and other personal expenses. Because they'll get four (or sometimes five) paychecks in a month, they won't get enough for rent from any one paycheck. Bi-weekly or twice a month works better for most employees on this regard.

Paying Twice a Month vs. Every Two Weeks

If you haven't really focused on this question before, you might think that every two weeks and two times a month works out the same. It doesn't. And the difference can kill your cash flow.

There are 52 weeks in a year and 13 weeks in a quarter. So, if you pay every two weeks, you have an extra pay period every now and then. Paying twice a month, you will have 24 pay periods in a year. Paying every two weeks, you will have 26 pay periods in a year. That means there will be two quarters (and more importantly, two months) with an "extra" pay period.

The totals come out the same for both employee and employer. But that extra pay period can be hard on the employer who doesn't have the discipline to set aside an extra sum every week to have the cash on hand. If you forget about it, or don't plan for it, then you have to come up with an extra payroll twice a year.

Ouch.

"Pay Period" and Pay Day

The next topic to look at is scheduling the lag time between end of pay period and payday. For example, if you pay weekly, you will probably end the pay period at end of day Friday or end of day Saturday (although it could be any time/day). You will need at least a week to collect time cards, make sure they're accurate, ask the employees to make corrections, and then process the actual payroll. So, with a little work, you could distribute checks one week later on Friday.

For example, you might schedule pay dates like this:

Period January 1-7 will be paid Friday 13

Period January 8-14 will be paid Friday 20

Period January 15-21 will be paid Friday 27

etc.

If you have pay periods of 1st to 15th and 16th to end of month, then you will also need at least a week until payday, but the actual pay date will vary because you have to worry about weekends. For example, if your goal is to pay around the 10th and 25th, you might occasionally move a pay date as follows:

Period January 1-15 will be paid on Wednesday Jan 25th

Period January 16-31 will be paid on Friday Feb 10th

Period February 1-15 will be paid on Friday Feb 24th (because the 25th is a Saturday)

We tried to pay on the 5th and 20th for a while, but we moved to the 10th and 25th for two reasons. First, the time frame was too short. Because two-day weekends can show up anywhere in the pay cycle, we usually did not have five days to settle time cards and process payroll.

Second, there is a serious cash flow issue with paying on the 5th. We run all managed services payments by credit card on the 1st of the month. Some process more quickly than others. This depends on whether the client is using American Express, Visa, or MasterCard. Generally, the money is available to us on the third business day after the 1st. Because of weekends, the third business day might be as late at the 6th. And, because we have so many holidays moved to Monday in the U.S., that means that the actual payday is moved as late as the 7th.

As a result, we had lots of pay dates where we were apologizing to employees and delaying the payday a day or two. In addition, most employees have rent due on the first, and it's late on the 5th. So getting paid on the 6th or 7th is a real hassle for them.

We solved this by simply moving payday to the 10th and 25th. That gives us plenty of time to let all the credit cards settle. Now our official policy is that pay days are on the 1st and 25th, and that "Saturday" pay days are paid on Friday and "Sunday" pay days are paid on Monday. This creates a pay period right **before** rent is due.

Payroll Services

Payroll services (Paychex, ADP, your accountant, etc.) are pretty good at helping you figure out what you need to do to get payroll scheduled. Some of them take the money out of your account the minute you hit ENTER. Others take the money the next day. A few will let you schedule a day 1-2 days out.

In all cases, these services will have standard operating procedures that help you stay compliant with your local and state laws regarding payroll. Every state is different, and a few localities add more regulations.

Implementation Notes

Implementing your pay roll procedure is pretty straight forward. You need to decide what works best for you, define it in a one-page memo to employees, and then document the process of actually processing it online with your payroll service.

I think it's a good idea to print out a list of holidays and pay dates for your employees each year, and distribute these during the first week of January. Remember, some "holidays" are not recognized by most businesses and banks (e.g., Groundhog Day in the U.S.). Other "holidays" are recognized by banks but not most businesses (e.g., Columbus Day in the U.S.). Overall, you just need to let your employees know what to expect.

Once you find a pay day schedule that works for you, it should just work smoothly. The only hard part might be moving from one pay schedule to another. Employees are rightfully nervous about losing a little money during a switch like this. So be sensitive to that.

If you're a managed service provider, you might find our system works well for you. Basically, we pay on the 10th and 25th, which is good for us and our employees. We like the 10th because it gives plenty of time for the credit cards to settle into our bank account from the first. Employees appreciate the 25th because it puts a paycheck in their pocket right before rent is due on the 1st.

Three Take-Aways from This Chapter:

1. Because payroll is the biggest piece of your budget, it is also the biggest element in your cash flow calculation.
2. Paying twice a month is generally easier to plan for than every two weeks – you avoid those two surprise payrolls each year.
3. Consider both your employees' cash flow and the company's cash flow.

Three Action Steps for Your Company:

1. ______________________________

____

2. ______________________________

____

3. ______________________________

____

26

Vendor Management and Coordination

One of the things you hear all the time with Managed Services is that you should manage the client's vendors. What exactly does that mean? What is "vendor management?" Well . . .

First, let's define what we mean by a vendor. By "vendor" we mean anyone that provides an important service or product to your clients, and that product or service is somehow related to the technology your support.

For example:

- QuickBooks, Business Works, MAS 90
- Line of Business applications (LOBs) such as IMIS, Dentrix, PC Law, Rent Manager, etc.
- Internet Service Providers
- Domain registrars
- Web developers
- Offsite storage companies
- Product supplies such as Dell, HP, or CDW

The reality is: Most of the time, you will never deal with these folks. Except Dell. If you sell and support Dell hardware, being on the phone with Dell is a regular part of your job. If you sell HP or Lenovo, you need to make sure you really document the support process very well because you will use it so rarely that you won't remember the process.

Anyway.

Most of the time, you don't deal with these vendors. So taking over "management" of them is very easy, because there's no labor involved. But there are some key points at which it is critical that you manage these relationships.

There are four important points at which you need to control or be involved in the vendor relationship. Most of this activity actually has to do with *documentation* and taking care of the little stuff that the client will never properly manage for themselves.

1. Buying and registering software

It is critically important that client software and products be properly registered to the client - and that you have access to this information and relationship. And, to be honest, it's important that you have standard processes so this information is available when there are personnel changes (including yourself). See the chapter "Activating and Registering Client Software and Hardware" in Volume Three of this series.

But it is also important that you be involved in the purchasing decision whenever possible. There are products that work well together. There are products that have good cloud integrations and products with bad cloud integrations. Many LOBs appear to be reasonably priced but require hundreds – or thousands – of hours of customization. You need to be the client's advocate in making these decisions.

Unless you have a very tight niche, you can't be familiar with every line of business app out there. But your technical ability will allow you to ask some questions, and report the answers at a level that will help the client make better decisions than they could on their own.

2. Interpreting the language

We are a little flippant when we tell clients that "we speak nerd-to-nerd" with vendors. But it's true. No matter how arcane the technology is, you are 100% more qualified to understand it and make good decisions than your client.

And vendors know this. Whether it's with sales or tech support, they can talk to you at a higher level regarding database structures, importing and exporting processes, file locations, permissions, etc. Vendors are used to helping end users through certain procedures, but it goes a LOT faster if you're involved.

3. When technical support is required

. Obviously, the problem will be solved faster and more accurately with you on the phone rather than the end user. The key thing here is that YOU are in charge of their access to the client computers. You are in charge of when things are done. And you need to monitor it.

There's also the question of Rules of Engagement. Are you using a service contract paid for by the client (e.g., product warranty), or a contract paid for by you (e.g., an "incident" as a Microsoft Certified Partner [or whatever they call it now])? What is your procedure for each of these? Document it!

4. Managing important information

I can't count how many times we've had to straighten out documentation because no one knows the ISP, or the web hosting service, or the relevant passwords for these services. Or the code that gets you the platinum weekend service.

Or critical products and services are registered in the name of a former employee, or a former IT support company. It goes on and on. And the bad news is that this situation will get worse. Business owners (and their employees, and their tech support people), address a problem by finding some random product on the Internet, buy it, and never record any critical information. So when they need it again, they can't access it (even if they remember the product name). Young people moving into the business world were raised with this approach to technology.

You need to have very standard procedures regarding documentation. It should be registered in the company's name with the administrator's email. That way, no matter what personnel changes occur, someone will still have access to the key information. Even if the owner dies. Even if a new tech support company comes in. Documentation, documentation, documentation.

Are You On The Clock?

One of the key questions in vendor management is the line you need to draw between "covered" and "billable" with regard to managed services. This is actually kind of a big picture question.

We include vendor management in our Platinum plan for one simple reason: When our goal is to cover everything AND reduce the cost of doing so, vendor management saves us more time (money) than it costs. That means that we almost never charge for anything related to vendors (tech support, service coordination, or monitoring work they have to do.).

As with all of our managed service plans, we do still charge for adds, move, and changes. That means that we can charge for labor related to major version upgrades and selecting new vendors. But we're very honest about giving away the hours related to supporting the existing setup.

Just as with any managed service, you need to draw the line as clearly as possible. You and your client both need to understand it. Luckily, unlike general tech support, most of your team will never have to make these decisions around vendor management. It is something for the owner and service manager to deal with.

For the most part, we give away the hours related to vendor management for two reasons. First, controlling all this stuff reduces our labor costs quite significantly. So we need to make it easy for the client to say yes to vendor management. It helps us support hardware, software, and services. In most cases we were going to have to engage 3rd party tech support for certain items anyway.

Second, we really want to "own" the relationship with the vendor. We want to know their processes, procedures, and tools. We want to know how they approach things. We want to gain knowledge that we can take to other clients, which makes us more valuable.

It's kind of interesting to contemplate: The client can never gain as much as we can from working with a vendor. We can solve things faster than the client because we understand geek-speak. And making the line of business apps work smoothly results in a happy client whose whole operation works better. If we're rigorous about documenting the process, the client has a better overall support system.

So everyone wins. There is no down side.

Do You Control Everything?

Some advisers say you should have ultimate authority to choose vendors. They say you should literally be able to select which $150,000 line of business app the client will use.

I would never go that far.

Some decisions, like which anti-virus program we install, are pretty trivial. We've reached the point where 99% of the AV companies are 99% the same as all the others. So we install what we think makes sense for us. Our price list mentions spam filtering, anti-virus, and RMM (remote monitoring and management) without regard to specific brand names. And we have changed vendors as needed for *our* purposes without consulting the client.

But I would never presume to be the one to make a huge LOB decision on behalf of the client. I want to be involved. But I don't want to make that decision.

The biggest client we ever had paid us almost exactly $150,000 per year. (We fired them. Long story. Great decision.) But most of our clients pay somewhere around $1,000 to $8,000 per month. So I don't want to make decisions on their behalf that exceeds what they pay us in a year!

For us the line is pretty straight forward: In all areas where direct communication makes our job easier, we want to be involved. Where the client needs high level advice about a decision that will cost lots of money, we want to be the adviser and not the decision maker.

Obviously, in all of this you need to decide what's best for your company. And document it!

Note: The next chapter discusses vendor record keeping. In Volume Four of this series we have two chapters on the specifics of working with third party tech support.

Three Take-Aways from This Chapter:

1. Managing the vendors without clients in between will save you money and hassles.
2. You need to draw clear lines between what's covered and what's billable when dealing with a client's vendors.
3. Wherever possible, you should be involved in advising clients about vendors, even if you choose not to be a decision-maker.

Three Action Steps for Your Company:

1. ____

2. ____

3. ____

27

Vendor/Distributor Record Keeping

In a perfect world, everything you need is available electronically, and is easy to search through. So when you need information, it's only a click or two away.

We don't live in that world.

Distributors (Ingram Micro, Synnex, D&H, etc.) are getting better at making information from past purchases available. But this is an area where you can create a very simple, very low-tech solution for tracking the information you need.

First, let's look at the information you need to keep and track.

Let's say you have two primary distributors, such as Ingram and D&H. But occasionally you buy RAM from the Crucial web site or software from CDW's reseller program. In the buying process, you might send purchase orders, receive invoices, and receive packing slips with merchandise.

This information is easily divided into two types: Financial information and merchandise information.

Financial information is primarily tracked through your QuickBooks or other finance tool. Once any disputes are settled, you will probably never need this information again. If you do need it, you'll find it in your system.

Merchandise information is more specific to the items you buy and sell. This is an interesting collection of information that you rarely need. But when you do need it, having it at your fingertips is priceless. For example, you might have a complete list of serial numbers on a packing slip. Or you might have all kinds of detailed information about a server install.

The papers you'll find with these juicy bits of information are primarily invoices and packing slips. Again, invoices might be available electronically, but not easily available electronically.

You might create a process to scan all these documents into your PSA or into client folders on your SharePoint site. But I don't recommend that. The truth is that you will rarely use these documents, so it's probably not worth creating a lot of work. Keep the documents you already have in paper format and don't fret about the rest.

Here's what I recommend.

1) Whenever you pay an invoice from a distributor, stamp it PAID and write the check number (or other payment information) on it.

2) Whenever you receive a packing slip that includes information you might find useful, add it to the file system.

3) Three-hole punch each of these documents and place them in a binder in chronological order.

If you have a low volume of product sales, you might keep all of these in one binder with a tab for each distributor. If you have a higher volume, you would dedicate one binder for each distributor.

Keep each binder for four years. Then shred the contents.

Using this Information

Here are a few examples of how we've used this information:

- When ordering hard drives to match or replace existing hard drives, we can quickly find the exact items ordered.
- When we want to refresh our memories about the server we sold three years ago so we know what we're replacing, we can go to the month of the sale and find all the related product descriptions.
- When there's a debate or discussion about when a warranty was purchased, or the type of warranty purchased, we can go right to the invoice.

Generally speaking, it works like this: Mike asks me what kind of drives are in a server we sold three or four years ago. I start by looking in QuickBooks. Since I know the client, there aren't many large hardware purchases to go through. I find the month of purchase and the invoice numbers for the distributor.

At this point, I simply open the binder for that distributor and flip to the month. I find the invoices within a minute or so. There I see the drive form factor, size, and speed. In fact, I have serial numbers in case that information is useful.

This process takes about five minutes in QuickBooks and about two minutes with the paper binders.

We probably use this information about once or twice a month. So it's not worth putting a huge effort into. If we didn't do this, we'd have a scavenger hunt once or twice a month.

This process is best left to whoever handles most of the product ordering for your company. But you need to make sure that technicians and whoever opens shipments pass the packing slips to this person for filing.

Obviously, you will need to fine-tune this SOP for your organization. Just make sure you keep it as streamlined as possible. Don't make it complicated or labor-intensive.

Three Take-Aways from This Chapter:

1. Invoices and packing slips can contain some juicy information. Put it where you can find it.
2. You probably don't need an all-electronic system since you rarely access this information.
3. When replacing or upgrading a server, being able to reconstruct exactly what you sold three years ago can be very handy.

Three Action Steps for Your Company:

1. ____

____

2. ____

____

3. ____

____

28

Inventory Management

There are a handful of things that can kill your cash flow and your profitability. One of them is inventory. Assuming you are not a store front, you need to keep inventory under control. There are three ways that inventory can kill you.

Note: I assume here that you are not running an actual store, so you don't need shelves full of inventory.

Many of us are creatures of habit. That means we do things the way we've always done them. Or we learn from someone else but don't really know why it's done that way. But that's the way we do it, so that's the way we do it.

With inventory, we used to keep quite a bit of stuff on hand. When I started my business in 1995, hard drives failed. So we kept a few hard drives on hand. We built our own systems, so we kept power supplies and memory on hand.

But there were different kinds of hard drives. IDE and at least three kinds of SCSI. And they all cost a lot of money. There were also different kinds of power supplies. Yes, the form factor didn't change that often, but you still had to keep something on hand for the installed base. Memory has always been a quickly-shifting world.

In all of these – plus modems, mother boards, network cards, CPUs, CPU Fans, etc. – we found ourselves with current stock and outdated stock. And when a specific form factor simply disappeared, we were stuck with 1-2 items that we would never sell. So now we had 10 or 12 memory chips, a couple of small hard drives, some ribbon cables, 5-6 various fans, and lots of other little stuff that would never sell.

Every once in a while we'd gather up all the old crap that was "brand new" but out of date and donate it to Goodwill or the local Indian reservation's ewaste program. Parallel cables. 5-Pin DIN keyboards. DAT3 tapes. Memory, memory, memory.

The first way that inventory kills your profit is tying up cash. Inventory costs money. A little here. A little there. Pretty soon you have $2,000 invested in things you will never sell. Of course you don't know you'll never sell them. They were originally "cost of goods sold." But they were never sold.

Now you see $2,000 worth of stuff go to the ewaste program and realize you could have bought yourself a really nice stereo instead!

In everything you buy for your business, you need to have a Return on Investment (ROI) calculation. Some things are true expenses, like office supplies. Some things are Cost of Goods Sold (COGS). But when you buy things for resale and never sell them, that's a write-off.

The second way that inventory kills your profit is that it has to be paid for with profit, not just money you have lying around. Let's look at some detail.

Let's say you have an EBITDA (Earnings Before Interest, Taxes, Depreciation and Amortization) of 10%. That means that you have to sell $100 worth of product to buy $10 worth of inventory. But wait. We were looking at $1,000 or $2,000 worth of inventory. That means you're tying up the profit from $10,000 or $20,000 worth of sales!!!

You need SOME inventory. Just be real clear about how much.

The third way that inventory kills your profit is returns and RMAs. Even if you get pre-paid for hardware and software, there will always be the occasional return. Returns cost time, and that's money. Whether it's the client who changed their mind or the product that arrived dead, you have to do whatever it takes to make it right.

You should calculate over time how much you spend on returns. It is not zero. So realistically, what do you spend on returns?

We have found that making clients prepay for everything has dramatically reduced returns.

In addition, we found that selling brand-name business class hardware with a three-year warranty has essentially eliminated RMAs (return merchandise authorizations) and DOAs (dead on arrivals).

So ...

This is not a policy or procedure that you need to talk about with all employees. But among the administrative and office staff, you should make it clear that you will work to keep inventory as low as possible.

It's a horrible feeling to realize that you spent good money on something that you need to throw away. But if you're conscious of the fact that you're doing this, it will help you realize that you need to minimize it going forward.

Keeping Inventory for Strategic Reasons

In general, I recommend that very small businesses avoid keeping inventory of any significant size. But there are times when keeping inventory is good for your business – even if you don't run a store.

In Volume Three of this series we'll discuss the technician's "scary" box. That's a small box of supplies that technicians might carry around. Over the years this has included network cards, modems, various cables, and other small items that are just handy to have on hand.

Of even greater strategic significance is the ability to keep larger items in stock. For example, if you sell a lot of certain computers or routers, it might be handy to keep one on the shelf ready to deliver. That takes delivery time from a few days to a few hours.

You may also decide to keep stock of supplies such as toner or monitors. These can give you an edge against other suppliers and make you look great to your clients.

But just be sure that you keep accurate track of your expenses! If you keep a $150 monitor on the shelf for very long, it will become a $125 monitor and you won't make any money. Plus you'll tie up your cash in inventory. Similarly, if the only client with a specific printer stops buying toner from you, you could be stuck with expensive supplies you'll never sell.

You need to decide how much inventory is right for your business. I recommend that you keep it as small as possible unless you have a strong strategic reason to do otherwise.

Three Take-Aways from This Chapter:

1. Old inventory can become worthless very quickly.
2. You never buy inventory with "cash flow." You buy inventory with profit.
3. Keep inventory as low as possible unless you have a strategic reason to do otherwise.

Three Action Steps for Your Company:

1. ______________________________

____

2. ______________________________

____

3. ______________________________

____

29

Is This a Profitable Hour?

From time to time, it's good to sit your staff down and teach them this mantra: "Is this a profitable hour for our company?"

In the KPEnterprises Standards and Procedures manual, it looks like this:

The KPEnterprises Mantra

Is this a profitable hour for KPEnterprises?

and shortly after that we have:

Work Ethics and Core Beliefs

- We strive for continuous improvement to all of our processes to ensure a high standard of work delivered.
- The best way to work is to focus on one thing completely and, when it is done or at a stopping point, move on to the next thing.
- Only change focus or allow distraction to the one thing you are doing if that interruption is directly related to the success or completion of the task at hand.

- All things can wait or be handled by someone else if their current status is correctly recorded for others to access. That is to say, if the PSA is up to date with notes, etc., anyone else with the correct technical ability can take over that Service Request or help it move forward toward resolution.
- We get all the information the first time and document it.
- We do complete work the first time around. No rework.
- The client you are currently servicing is the most important client right now.
- We complete all work possible before leaving a client's office.

Not everything on that list is directly related to profitability, but everything in the entire company is at least indirectly related to it.

In Volume Two of this series we'll look at the Roles and Responsibilities for the service manager and for technicians. In both cases, you'll see the line

"Focus on making every work hour a profitable hour for KPE."

Everyone's In On This!

No matter how large or small your company is, every employee needs to keep an eye on profitability. Of course many of them will not see a direct line between their daily activities and the profitability of the company. That means it's up to you to draw the lines for them.

For example, administrative assistants need to know that their work helps marketing efforts, which leads to sale, which leads to money that runs the whole company.

The front office staff do a lot of work with billing, mailings, and finances. So even though they don't perform billable labor, they do all the hard work that actually brings the money in so the company can operate. And sometimes they do a better job of this than the owner! For example, it is very common that the owner will give discounts and forgive bills from time to time. That happens a lot less when billing is turned over to the front office staff.

Sales people obviously understand the connection between their success and the company's success.

The tech department - the service delivery department - has the strongest connection between their daily activities and the profitability of the company. In fact, they're the only employees who are evaluated on the basis of how "billable" they are.

When you break down a technician's hour, it might contain several activities, such as

- Check the service board
- Work tickets (deliver service)
- Read email
- Perform administrative duties
- Training / studying for exams
- Taking exams
- Attend meetings
- Wasting time on Facebook, dilbert.com, and YouTube

Most of these are either known to be profitable (billable labor is still considered "billable" if it is productive labor in support of a prepaid managed service agreement) or administrative. One of the reasons 60-70% billability is acceptable is that you expect technicians to read email, learn new technologies, and attend meetings.

The hidden culprits to profitability are not in the hours spent in each of the categories. The hidden culprits have to do with actual job performance and skills. For example, rework is extremely expensive for I.T. companies. If work is not properly documented, the chances for rework go way up. If a technician is thrown into a job with insufficient training, the probability for rework goes way up.

Inefficient troubleshooting is also a huge time waster. That's why we have a rule that the maximum time anyone should work on any problem before stopping and calling for feedback or support is 30 minutes. It is extremely important that technicians do not waste time continually trying the same thing over and over and expecting new results. Sometimes they just need a "fresh pair of eyes" on the problem. Sometimes they need to escalate to vendor support or other third party support.

Very often, we geeks refuse to give up. We won't let a USB device defeat us! So we want to keep working until we fix the problem. That's great if you're a sole proprietor and your time is worth nothing. But when you have employees, this can get very expensive very fast.

One time I had a tech who spent four hours working on a cell phone issue, making no progress. Then, after one six minute call to the Sprint store, it was fixed. Lesson learned. I can't charge a client for four hours labor. But I have to pay the technician. This is a losing proposition in at least three ways.

1) We look incompetent. That doesn't cost money right away, but it certainly can in the long run.

2) At about $25/hour with taxes, that tech's labor cost me $100.

3) More importantly, that's four hours we did not bill out in productive labor. At the time, our rate was $120/hr, which adds up to $480.

(That was about ten years ago and may actually be the reason we implemented the 30 minute limit.)

Productive Labor

Even technicians don't have to think in terms of dollars when they evaluate whether the hour is profitable. Rather, they can consider whether their actions are productive. Are they moving a ticket toward completion, or spinning their wheels? Is time better spent finding the cause of a problem or simply fixing it? Does this action advance the goals of the company with regard to client relationships or service department goals?

And so forth.

It is also critical that employees see how their actions fit in the big picture. For example, technicians often say that entering time and notes into the PSA is wasteful. They see it as bureaucratic activity and not productive labor. Very often, that's because they do not enter time into the ticket as soon as it's completed. When the last thing you do on a ticket is enter the notes, that activity is part of the ticket. When you wait until the end of the day, or the next day, that activity is administrative catch-up.

More importantly, accurate notes at time of service help us avoid rework. They help the service manager answer questions from a client as soon as the job is complete - and not have to wait until the next day when notes are in the system. Accurate notes also help the front office produce accurate billing. And they help whoever does customer service to justify the bill if a client has a question.

It is worthwhile to bring up the topic "Is this a profitable hour for the company?" at least once or twice a year in your company meetings. No one should obsess over it, but everyone should think about it.

Profitability doesn't just happen.

Productivity doesn't just happen.

Three Take-Aways from This Chapter:

1. If work is not properly documented, the chances for rework go way up.
2. Every employee plays some role in the profitability of the company.
3. All technician activity is either moving a ticket toward completion or not moving a ticket toward completion.

Three Action Steps for Your Company:

1. ______________________________________

   ____

2. ______________________________________

   ____

3. ______________________________________

   ____

30

Financial Goals: More than Revenue Targets

In the next two chapters we'll talk revenue projections and getting started with financial goals. But first, let's look beyond the money. This isn't quite a "mission statement" discussion, but it's not too far off of that either.

I like to remind small business owners: **Your business exists to serve your personal goals.** Yes you want to make money. Yes you want to help clients. But what's the big picture?

One of the terms you might hear in management training is "stakeholder." This is different from a stockholder. A stock holder owns a piece of the company. A stake holder has a stake in the company. Stakeholders include the owners, the managers, the employees, the clients, and even the vendors.

Now that doesn't mean you need to intentionally create a business for the benefit of all those folks. But you should take stock of who they are. Let me tell you a story about a client who is a great stakeholder in our company.

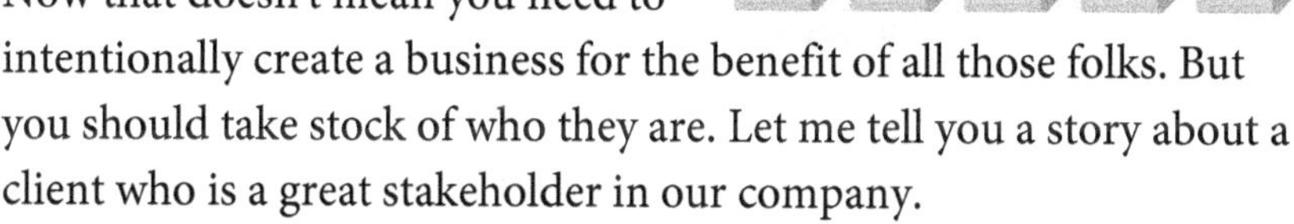

One day Mike and I were talking about this client and trying to decide whether to charge them for an onsite visit that consisted of turning on a switch. I put my labor as standard on site labor. That means billable. Then I told Mike he has to decide whether or not to charge an hour for that.

Mike said "No. First, it's [Company]. Second, it's Janet. Third, they always do everything we say. In fact, they bought a new server before the three year warranty was expired on the last server."

On two different occasions we almost dropped this client because they were below our 10-user threshold. They literally begged us not to drop them. They honestly see our support as a key element in their success.

That's a stakeholder!

Now, what has all that to do with setting your financial goals? It's simple: Making money is also about being happy, making your clients happy, making your employees happy, and keeping your vendors happy. So when you sit down to project targets for the next year, three years, and five years, you should take all that into account.

There is a true cost – a monetary cost – to having loyal clients and loyal employees. It might mean keeping smaller clients, paying employee benefits, or even throwing a party once in a while. Sometimes you need to budget for "unnecessary" expenses that make your company a better place to work and a better company to do business with.

And it's not selfish to consider your personal goals as well. What do you want to do with your life? Do you want to travel more? Buy some rental property? Start a non-profit organization? Put your kids through college?

Also consider the long-term goals of the business itself. What's the "end game" strategy? I was talking to a good friend about a very esoteric part of my business and trying to decide on pricing strategies.

In true entrepreneurial style he asked me what effect this decision would have on selling my business (Small Biz Thoughts). We had never talked about me selling this business, but he assumed that that's one possible end game. And he wisely suggested that I make decisions based on the long-term goals of the company.

Let's be honest: Most clients are really just customers. Most employees are not in it for the long haul. Most vendors don't really care much at all about your business. But some clients are true stakeholders. Some employees are true stakeholders. And even some vendors might be stakeholders.

All of this ties into the discussion of the kind of company you want to be. We work hard to have employees and clients who are fun to work with. I love it when employees say "I love my job." And I'm proud to say I've heard that many, many times in my life.

It takes intention to create a business that serves your goals – personal and professional. First you need to acknowledge these goals. Then you need to keep them top of mind as you plan out your budget for the next year. Some of these things cost money. But in the long run they create the company you want.

Nothing happens by itself.

Three Take-Aways from This Chapter:

1. Do you run a company you would like to work at? You should!
2. Your business exists to help you fulfill your personal goals.
3. Employees and clients will be far more committed if they feel they are stakeholders in your business.

Three Action Steps for Your Company:

1. ______________________________

____

2. ______________________________

____

3. ______________________________

____

31

Financial Goals: Realistic Revenue Projections

I maintain a spreadsheet of the basic profit and loss of my company month by month. So I have a picture of where my money came from and went to in January, February, March, etc. I start out with all of the months filled with projections. Then, as each month becomes real, I replace projections with real numbers.

(If you want to see a sample of this, download the sample Excel spreadsheet and related materials that accompany this book. This included with the Free Business Plan Resources mentioned in Chapter sixteen. Register this book at www.SMBBooks.com.)

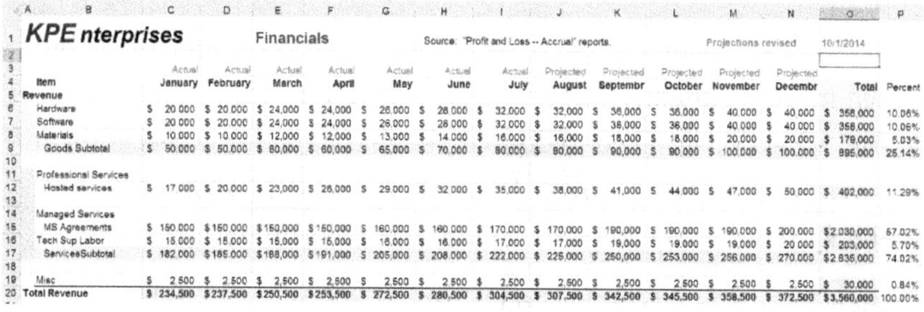

KPE nterprises Financials Source: "Profit and Loss -- Accrual" reports. Projections revised 10/1/2014

Item	Actual January	Actual February	Actual March	Actual April	Actual May	Actual June	Actual July	Projected August	Projected Septembr	Projected October	Projected November	Projected Decembr	Total	Percent
Revenue														
Hardware	$ 20,000	$ 20,000	$ 24,000	$ 24,000	$ 26,000	$ 28,000	$ 32,000	$ 32,000	$ 36,000	$ 36,000	$ 40,000	$ 40,000	$ 358,000	10.06%
Software	$ 20,000	$ 20,000	$ 24,000	$ 24,000	$ 26,000	$ 28,000	$ 32,000	$ 32,000	$ 36,000	$ 36,000	$ 40,000	$ 40,000	$ 358,000	10.06%
Materials	$ 10,000	$ 10,000	$ 12,000	$ 12,000	$ 13,000	$ 14,000	$ 16,000	$ 16,000	$ 18,000	$ 18,000	$ 20,000	$ 20,000	$ 179,000	5.03%
Goods Subtotal	$ 50,000	$ 50,000	$ 60,000	$ 60,000	$ 65,000	$ 70,000	$ 80,000	$ 80,000	$ 90,000	$ 90,000	$ 100,000	$ 100,000	$ 895,000	25.14%
Professional Services														
Hosted services	$ 17,000	$ 20,000	$ 23,000	$ 26,000	$ 29,000	$ 32,000	$ 35,000	$ 38,000	$ 41,000	$ 44,000	$ 47,000	$ 50,000	$ 402,000	11.29%
Managed Services														
MS Agreements	$ 150,000	$ 150,000	$ 150,000	$ 150,000	$ 160,000	$ 160,000	$ 170,000	$ 170,000	$ 190,000	$ 190,000	$ 190,000	$ 200,000	$2,030,000	57.02%
Tech Sup Labor	$ 15,000	$ 15,000	$ 15,000	$ 15,000	$ 16,000	$ 16,000	$ 17,000	$ 17,000	$ 19,000	$ 19,000	$ 19,000	$ 20,000	$ 203,000	5.70%
ServicesSubtotal	$ 182,000	$ 185,000	$ 188,000	$ 191,000	$ 205,000	$ 208,000	$ 222,000	$ 225,000	$ 250,000	$ 253,000	$ 256,000	$ 270,000	$2,635,000	74.02%
Misc	$ 2,500	$ 2,500	$ 2,500	$ 2,500	$ 2,500	$ 2,500	$ 2,500	$ 2,500	$ 2,500	$ 2,500	$ 2,500	$ 2,500	$ 30,000	0.84%
Total Revenue	$ 234,500	$ 237,500	$ 250,500	$ 253,500	$ 272,500	$ 280,500	$ 304,500	$ 307,500	$ 342,500	$ 345,500	$ 358,500	$ 372,500	$3,560,000	100.00%

Sample Revenue Projection

In the last few months of the year, I start working on the projections for next year. What do we expect in project labor, managed services, hardware, software, hosting, etc.? I fill in numbers for each month. And, of course, we project some growth for the new year. See the sample display of revenue projections. Notice that it moves from "projected" to "actual" in August. Of course these are all fictional numbers.

In the next chapter we'll talk about basic financial goals. But actual revenue projections take a different view of the future. I am a firm believer that every business should have a one year, a three year, and a five year projection of where you want to go. For most businesses, anything beyond that is wild speculation.

In fact, five years might be wild speculation. But three years should be based in reality and should be attainable. The one year plan should be very realistic and reflect what you really expect. Here's what I mean.

If you set a goal of doubling your business in twelve months, that might be possible. It might be very realistic. Or it might be completely impossible. You want to stretch your goals, but not to the point where they're simply fiction.

So let's say you want to have 20% growth. That's still aggressive, but much more attainable. Okay, so how will you get there? In the real world, what do you need to do to make that happen? In December of this year you make $X, and in December of next year you expect to make $X*1.2. What's the action plan that gets you there?

Somewhere from December to December you're going to have to demonstrate an increase in one or more types of revenue. What drives that increase? Tell me the story of how you will do that.

Luckily, in managed services, we can plot and plan to increase recurring revenue. So the narrative (the story that supports this projection) needs to say something like

- Add one $500/month managed service contract per month

or

- Add one $5,000/month manage service contract per quarter

The next question is: How realistic is that? Have you been able to sell one small client per month or one large client per quarter? If so, great. If not, then explain how you are going to do that next year. It might be very real. You might have a grand marketing plan and you just hired a new sales person. Just make sure that there's a realistic "how" behind your ambitious plan.

Here are some basic questions to ask that will keep your revenue projections realistic:

The best estimate of next year's performance is this year's performance.

Unless you can tell me why that's not true. This year might have had an extraordinary event that simply won't happen next year (good or bad).

I had a stretch of about ten years when I signed about one new client every calendar quarter. Some were large, some were small. Sometimes I dropped small clients to serve the new, larger clients. Sometimes I hired staff. Both of those events have to be accounted for. Bumping up the revenue by $1,000/month, followed by bumping up the payroll expense by $4,000/month can both be accomplished. But they need to be in the context of a realistic larger picture.

Your future budget must start with where you are right now.

You cannot "assume" a brighter January unless you have a plan to make that happen. From today – from this month – you can tell a story of how you'll gain clients. If you start from today, you will ground your predictions in reality.

Be clear about your assumptions for next year.

What do you think the economy will do? Why do you think that? What changes will you make and when? Will you hire someone? Will you offer a new service? Will you raise your rates?

Make notes about your assumptions and plans in the margin of your Excel spreadsheet. For example "Assume two new managed services clients per month. Will hire new tech 20 hours/week in May." You don't need lengthy paragraphs, just enough to jog your memory about what you'll tell someone to justify your numbers. That someone might be your accountant, your spouse, or your service manager.

Keep the end in mind.

Now we're back to the long term. If you plan to double the size of your business in five years, what are the assumptions about years 1, 2, 3, and 4? If you're going to sell your business or retire in year five, what do you need to do between now and then to reach your goals? What has to change and what has to stay the same?

Short term and medium term goals should always move you toward your longer-term goals.

Share your projections and get feedback.

Show you budget projections to someone and ask them whether it looks realistic. You might be surprised with the questions you'll get.

Put your ego aside and try to answer their questions. If you can't, then you need to realistically re-evaluate your budget.

This might sound like a pain in the neck. But it really is an exercise worth doing. Even if you've been in business for ten years without a budget, I think you'll be surprised at the difference it makes when you do have a budget.

. . . Of course that assumes you pay attention to it once a month after the new year begins . . .

Three Take-Aways from This Chapter:

1. The best estimate of next year's performance is this year's performance. (Unless you can a story of why that's not true.)
2. You should create realistic 1, 3, and 5-year budget estimates.
3. Make realistic assumptions and tell good stories that demonstrate how real your projections are.

Three Action Steps for Your Company:

1. ______________________________

   ____

2. ______________________________

   ____

3. ______________________________

   ____

32

Financial Goals: Getting Started

Finances are fundamental to running a successful business. No matter whether you love finances or hate them, you have to take care of them. Not taking care of your finances can only result in one outcome: Losing money!

When most people think of financial goals they think of revenue projections. ("I made $335,000 this year and plan to make $400,000 next year.") But there are lots of other "basic" finances you need to set goals for. Here are a few thoughts.

Revenue

Okay. You need to have revenue projections. They need to be realistic. And you need to look at them often enough to KNOW them so you can reach them. After all, if you don't your goal for the month or the year, how could you possibly reach it except by accident?

Revenue is income: The total amount of money that you bring into the organization. Never confuse revenue with profit. They are related. And if you follow all the advice in this 4-book series you will be able to make some excellent guestimates of profit based on revenue. But they are not the same.

For example: Tesla Motors reported $620.5 million in revenue for the first quarter of 2014 – and a loss of $49.8 million. Obviously, their board feels the different between revenue and profit (loss).

Profit

Now we're talking money! Revenue is good, but profit is better. If you make $500,000 in revenue and only $100,000 in profit, that's worse that earning $350,000 and making $100,000 profit. The reason is simple: It takes a lot more work to earn that $500,000.

You should have profit goals for each month and for the year. So now you need both revenue goals and profit goals.

Profit Margin

Profit is often describe in dollars while margin is often described as a percentage. They come from the same numbers. Your profit margin is literally the connection between Revenue and Profit. You should have specific goals for each broad category of what you sell: Products, labor, services, etc.

Everyone has different recommendations for these goals. You need to set these goals yourself, but consider the following as a starting point. In my opinion, hardware and software should have a profit margin of 20%. Labor should be more like 40%. With managed services, you might push labor to 50%.

Services can be all over the map. For cloud services, we start with a 100% markup, which gives us a minimum of 50% profit margin. If you are providing a backup service, you can combine the service with your labor and maintenance for one price. If you do that, be sure to track the cost of service and related labor under "cost of goods sold" so that you calculate the profit margin.

Here's a quick demonstration of the relationship of profit to margin. Let's say you can buy a hard drive through distribution for $100. I recommend you mark it up 25%. That means you'll sell it for $125. Your profit is now $25 or 20% of the $125 sales price.

Here are the labels:

Cost of Goods Sold:	$100		
Markup:	$25	25%	
Revenue from Sale:	$125		
Income from Sale:	$125		
Margin:	$25	20%	of $125
Profit:	$25	20%	

EBITDA and EBITDA Percentage

EBITDA is "Earnings before interest, taxes, dividends, and amortization." For most small businesses, this is almost identical to net operating profit. Work with your accountant to verify the items you need to back out of your calculations (such as tax payments made) to calculate EBITDA from profit.

But here's the bottom line, so to speak. Your EBITDA Percentage should be a minimum of 8-10%. That is absolute minimum. It could easily get to 15% or even 20% or more. If you can't sustain eight percent, take your money out of your business and put it into the stock market. That will give you an average return around 8%.

Monthly and Annually

All of those numbers should be tracked monthly, in your PSA, QuickBooks, or both. I like to put all of that into a single Excel workbook so that I can track the "Year to Date" information. Sometimes you'll invoice a client in one month and then end up ordering the equipment (incurring the expense) in the next month. As a result, the first month will look more profitable than it should and the next month will look less profitable than it should. But the year to date stats will be correct after the 2nd month.

Anyway, you should have monthly targets for revenue and profit, primarily. Everything else flows from that. I recommend looking at your finance AT LEAST once a month. Ideally, you should do it every week on the same day. That gives you a good sense of how money flows in and out of your company.

As the year moves along, you should have two sets of numbers: The real numbers for months past and the projected numbers for the months ahead. And of course you'll have a final tally for the end of the year. As the year progresses, each month will move from "projected" to "actual" and your projection for the whole year will become clearer and clearer.

I know this sounds like a lot for the basics, but once you begin looking at these numbers all the time, it will be very easy to understand at a glance and won't take more time.

One of my favorite maxims of success is that you get better at whatever you put your attention on. If you put your attention on your finances, you will make more money. It just is true. And once you have goals for each month and the year as a whole, you can reach them as well.

Three Take-Aways from This Chapter:

1. Revenue is income. Don't confuse revenue and profit. Profit is more important.
2. Your net operating profit should be at least 8%.
3. Set standard mark-ups for goods and services. These (almost) guarantee profitability.

Three Action Steps for Your Company:

1. ______________________________

____

2. ______________________________

____

3. ______________________________

____

33

How to Track Credit Card Auto-Payments

One of the great benefits - and curses - of the 21st century is the "Auto-Payment" for goods and services. We use them to pay for all kinds of things. And we ask our clients to do the same.

The great advantage of auto-payments, of course, is that you don't forget a payment. And some services are only available with credit card or other auto-payment. The great disadvantage of auto-payments is that you can lose track of the total amount.

And the real major pain-in-the-neck disadvantage comes when your credit card expires. Or in these days of credit theft, we're seeing banks suspend credit cards for almost any suspicious activity. That's great for protecting your credit – unless it leads to missed payments for one or more auto-payments!

Here are a few tips to make your life easier.

Tracking Auto-Payments

The first thing you need to do is to create a spreadsheet of auto-payments for your business. See the example. It's also a good idea to track cards that are stored with online sites that allow you to make occasional payments. This is less important since you can change

	A	B	C	D	E	F	G	H	I	J
1	**Auto Payments - GLB**							**Cards on File With ...**		
2										
3	**Day of Month**	**Item / Service**	**Amount**		**Card / Account**	**Exp Date**		**Item / Service**	**Card / Account**	**Exp Date**
4	2	LinkedIn	$ 24.95		TCB 9775	11/2016		Amazon	Chase 1805	02/2017
5	2	Constant Contact	$ 80.00		Chase 1805	02/2017		Delta	TCB 2915	05/2015
6	2	Sharefile.com	$ 23.95		ACH			Kaiser	ACH	
7	3	Volusion	$ 102.74	*	TCB 2915	05/2015		Lightning Source	Chase 1805	02/2017
8	6	Presenterbox	$ 49.00		Chase 1805	02/2017		SRS Plus	Chase 1805	02/2017
9	6	Azure	$ 90.00	*	ACH			Travelocity	TCB 2915	05/2015
10	7	Boingo	$ 4.98		TCB 2915	05/2015		USPS	TCB 2915	05/2015
11	7	Dreamhost	$ 34.24	*	TCB 2915	05/2015				
12	7	GogoAir.com	$ 18.95		Chase 1805	02/2017				
13	11	Docusign	$ 24.99		TCB 2915	05/2015				
14	12	Adobe Cloud	$ 49.99		ACH					
15	13	Networked Blogs	$ 19.99		TCB 2915	05/2015				
16	14	Audible	$ 14.95		TCB 2915	05/2015				
17	17	Natomas Self Storage	$ 94.00		Chase 1805	02/2017				
18	28	Instant Teleseminar	$ 67.49		ACH					
19	31	Clickbank	$ 19.00		TCB 2915	05/2015				
20		**Monthly Total:**	**$ 719.22**							
21										
22				* Variable Amount						

these on a whim. But if someone in your company makes payments for you, you need to make sure the correct card is stored online.

Assuming you've already got a number of auto-payments scheduled, the first chore is to log these. The best place to find a complete list of payments you've already approved is your bank or credit card statement. Here's what you do:

1) Dig out bank statements and credit card statements for the last four months.

2) Open Excel and create a new spreadsheet with columns for the day of the month, the name of the service, the amount, and the credit/debit card used.

3) Look through your statements and mark each item that is a recurring payment.

4) Enter the recurring payments on your Excel spreadsheet. Enter the day of week on the appropriate column. Then look ahead for the same payment for the next month, and the next, and the next. Because of weekends, some payments will move around a bit. On the spreadsheet, keep the date that occurs the earliest for each item. This will come in handy someday if you want to use this information to assist in tracking your cash flow.

5) Keep an eye out for payments that recur once every two or three months. There will be fewer of these, so you need to be careful not to miss one. Of course there might also be one or two that recur once every six or twelve months. It's probably not worth looking through a year's worth of statements to find them all. See #6.

6) Make it a habit to verify auto-payments as they occur. That way, you can add the once-per-year and twice-per-year items to your tracking sheet.

7) Note that some items vary from month to month. Be sure to note these. If you enter the highest occurrence over the four month period, you'll have a safe budget.

8) Total the entries at the bottom. It never hurts to know what you've committed yourself to every month!

Minimizing Hassles with Auto-Payments

As I alluded to above, there are certain hassles with relying on credit cards for auto-payments. The same is true with debit cards (ATM cards). You need to decide whether you'll use credit cards, debit cards, direct ACH payments, or a combination of these. (ACH stands for Automated Clearing House - a system that enables you to make payments directly from your bank account.) You are most likely using a combination of these.

Credit cards are a good choice if you don't want to keep track of whether or not you have enough cash in the account at a given time. Debit cards are a good choice if you want to work on a "cash" basis. When a debit card is charged, the money goes straight out of your account. ACH is a good choice if you like to work on a cash basis like a debit card but don't want to worry about expiration dates.

Here's a quick summary of the hassles you should account for:

1) The biggest hassle you have to deal with is the expiration date for each card. If you don't keep on top of this, you'll have a spate of rejected payments. You can avoid this by moving to ACH payments, which don't have an expiration date. You can also avoid this by changing the card online as soon as you receive a new card. That's where this spreadsheet comes in real handy.

2) The other big hassle you'll have is when a card you're using is canceled or suspended due to suspicious activity. I've been a victim of

this myself. Two summers ago, the card I carry when I travel was canceled twice within a month. My travel isn't unusual at all for me, but the bank wanted to protect me. In addition to being a hassle on the road, I had to go put a number of payments onto a new card before the next charge hit.

This is becoming more and more common as banks get more and more skittish about fraud.

If you want to use a credit or debit card and avoid having it canceled due to travel or other activities, you should get a card you only use for online recurring payments. This could be a credit card with just enough of a credit line to cover the recurring payments. Or it could be a debit card that is never used for anything else. That's what I use.

Because the card never travels, it is never handled by unscrupulous waiters, it is never used at a store where the systems are compromised, and it never magically has transactions at gas stations in two different time zones on the same day.

Maintenance

Once you have a spreadsheet, it should be maintained by whoever manages your finances regularly. That might be you, the office manager, the bookkeeper, etc. Make sure new recurring payments are added to the list and old ones are removed.

The true benefit of keeping this tracking sheet will come when you change cards, change banks, or need to take a look at your budget for planning purposes. So, of course, whenever you make such changes, you need to make sure to update the Excel spreadsheet.

I recommend you keep the spreadsheet in your public folder under the \operations\finance folder.

A sample copy of this spreadsheet in Excel format is included with the downloadable material you receive with this book.

Three Take-Aways from This Chapter:

1. Auto-payments are awesome – until your credit card changes.
2. Create a spreadsheet of all credit card, debit, and ACH auto-payments. Keep it up to date.
3. As long as you've got it, use the auto-pay spreadsheet to get a sense of your monthly overhead. At least some of it.

Three Action Steps for Your Company:

1. ______________________________

____

2. ______________________________

____

3. ______________________________

____

Section III

Sales, Marketing, and Client Management

34

Defining Your Company to Clients and Employees

"Nice to meet you. So what do you do?"

Boring and uninspired networking blabber.

But nonetheless, you need an answer.

Ask your employees what your company does. You'll be amazed at the variety of answers. Most will be bumbling and stumbling. Something along the lines that you provide computer and network support that's the best in the business. Blah, blah, blah.

Someone might mention a thing called "managed services." Ugh. What's that? What does it cover? Listen to your staff. You probably won't like what you hear.

I know you've heard about **branding** and **30 second elevator speeches**. Well, here's a very simple process for defining and enforcing your branding. The hardest part is to define who you are and what you offer in 1-2 sentences each. Ideally, it will be one sentence to answer the question "What do you do?" and one sentence to answer the question "What is covered by managed services?"

Define Your Company

First, create your two simple answers. I use the word simple, but it can actually be quite a chore to boil down the essence of your business into one line. The goal here is to give your staff an answer they can memorize so thoroughly that it rolls off their lips.

At the grocery store. At holiday parties. At football games. Wherever. Whenever. Your goal is to craft a simple sentence that will roll off their lips automatically whenever the question arises: What do you do?

Your answer cannot be merely technical. You can't say "We maximize network efficiency to provide optimal strategic advantage for our clients." Yuck. This might be technically accurate, but it doesn't serve your company well. You need to craft a sentence that will 1) Answer the question; 2) Avoid boring or confusing the inquirer; and 3) Lead to additional questions. Number One is much more important than Number Two, and Number Two is far more important than Number Three.

What you don't want is a company at which every employee has a different definition of what you do and how you do it. So you need to create a one-sentence answer that gives an accurate (and positive) perception of your business, avoids technical jargon, and invites more interesting questions. All of your employees can answer the additional questions that follow from the simple introduction. You need to make sure you provide them with a quick answer that gets the conversation off to a good start.

Here's the line we use at KPEnterprises: **"We design, build, and support computer services for small businesses."**

We used to say that we design, build, and support Microsoft networks for small businesses. But we're a lot more open to non-Microsoft solutions than we were a few years ago.

We design, build, and support computer services for small businesses.

Everyone who hears this can understand it. Or at least they can understand enough to feel comfortable with it. They have a sense of what you do. They know you're not a plumber, a lawyer, or an accountant. You do something with computers and small businesses.

At this point, additional conversation is possible. There's a seed of something to talk about. What you've done is to create a positive image that is not misleading. You've provided information and avoided potential stumbling and fumbling that can mislead the listener.

There's one other minor advantage to having a clear, succinct branding: Your clients and prospects, if they hear this enough, may actually be able to inform others about what you do. Rather than being "The Computer Guy" you'll be the company that designs, builds, and supports computer services for small businesses.

Note on Networking: Networking is not sales. The goal here is NOT to make a sale. Your employees won't sell a managed service contract at a bar, waiting at the car wash, or at a Christmas party. So that's not the goal. The goal is to give them the right answer, and to avoid a stumbling answer.

Define Managed Services

As with your own company, the definition of managed services is very important. Some people have never heard of it. Some have misperceptions. Some are unsure about what's covered and what's not.

Unlike the description of what your company does, the definition of managed services is something that helps your employees and clients understand your business every day. What's covered and what's not? That's the question you need to answer in a simple sentence.

You can't use a big paragraph here. You need a simple sentence that you (and your employees, and your clients) can take apart and understand. It is literally the foundation of what you deliver under the title Managed Services.

Again, you need a well-crafted one sentence answer. Here's what we've used for years. If you've attended a seminar from me, or bought the recording, then you've heard it:

"*Managed Service covers the maintenance of the operating systems and software.*"

There are four levels of understanding here. This sentence works for all of them.

First, there are people whose eyes have already glossed over. Blah blah blah. Computer. Blah blah blah. This sentence simply allows them to nod and then move on to the cheese bits.

Second, a potential prospect, might engage in a deeper discussion. That allows you/your employee to describe the joys of flat fee pricing, preventive maintenance, etc.

Third, your employees need to be able to use this sentence to re-construct in their head the fine points of what's covered and what's not.

Fourth, this line allows your current customers to re-construct in their head the fine points of what's covered and what's not.

Here's what I mean by the last two items. Take that sentence apart. What's covered by managed services?

1) Maintenance . . . so NOT adds, moves, and changes.

2) Operating systems and software . . . so NOT hardware.

You might have all kinds of deals with hardware as a service, plans that cover network equipment, etc. But the 90% rule should be covered by your one-sentence description.

And, of course, what works for us might not work for you. So fine-tune, test, and create your own killer description.

Our one-sentence answer is not intended to replace a 14-page contract on managed services. But it allows us to start the conversation on the right foot. We can elaborate by saying, "Basically, if something is working and breaks, we fix it for free. If you want to add software, we'll charge for that. But once it works, then it's covered." Maintenance of the operating system and software.

Learning/Memorizing

So now you have two cool little sentences that you want everyone to memorize until they are automatic responses.

What do we do? *We design, build, and support computer services for small businesses.*

What's covered by managed services? *Managed Service covers the maintenance of the operating systems and software.*

Boom! Perfect.

Now you need to get some memorization out of the way. This is really not too difficult. First, you need to write out these sentences. Then you need to set up a system to test your employees . . . over and over again forever.

When we had a larger staff, we used to "test" on these phrases once a month. I would ask people to write down what we do, then read their answers out loud. It's AMAZING that people couldn't memorize these two sentences . . . sometimes after years with the company.

But that's why it's important to drill. First, if you don't drill, then you have no hope of being successful. You can't enforce what you don't measure. Basic Peter Drucker management stuff here.

So, you need to ask people to memorize. Then you need to "test" how well they're doing. Again and again.

Over time, everyone will get better. In our experience, administrative assistants did the best. They wrote out the phrases and posted them to their monitors. And when it came time for a test, they got it right. Technicians tended to be stumbling and say something different each time. And that's why you need to be consistent about this.

I do have to say: It is very gratifying to hear someone answer the phone and, after a brief interchange, casually say "We design, build, and support computer services for small businesses."

Implementation

There are no specific forms for implementing this SOP. You might write up your two sentences and distribute them to everyone. Post them publicly.

This process requires that everyone on the team

1) Be aware of the branding

2) Practice the branding

3) Correct one another's errors

4) Support one another with reminders

Three Take-Aways from This Chapter:

1. You need simple, clear, concise sentence to describe what your company does. You need the same for managed services.
2. Drive every employee until they get this right.
3. Use the definition of managed services all the time when you communicate internally or externally. Make it part of your company DNA.

Three Action Steps for Your Company:

1. ______________________________

   ____

2. ______________________________

   ____

3. ______________________________

   ____

35

Business Cards . . . All the Details

I find business cards very frustrating. Maybe 75% of the people with business cards should never have them because 1) They never need them due to the nature of their job, 2) They don't know how to use them, or 3) Their cards are almost useless.

On the first point, there are lots of people who just go to the office and are never out meeting people or representing the company. Other than to show their parents, or pass out as "dating cards," these people never use their business cards. So get them 100 or so and don't worry about the cost per card because they'll never need another 100.

How To Use A Business Card

(and Why Your Business Card Might be Useless)

At gatherings I sometimes collect business cards. Sometimes means only if I have a reason to. Believe it or not, I don't put everyone I've ever met on my mailing list. So when I collect a card I either intend to contact that person or (on occasion) I intend to add them to a list.

Here's an exercise:

- Take out your business card.

- Turn it over and write on the back. Here's what you write:

1=Small Biz Mixer

2=Kid in soccer league

3=Send seminar invite

If you can't write this on the back of your card, neither can anyone else! If that's the case, order new business cards.

If the back of your cards is glossy, throw them away and order new business cards. If the back of your card is covered with advertising or something else, throw them away and order new business cards.

I hear this ridiculous advice over and over: "You should use the back of your business card (so it's not wasted)." Bullshit. You should leave the back of your card empty enough for me to write critical information on.

As someone who really uses the cards I collect, I want that space on the back of every card. You can use some of the space for YOU (info, logo, QR code, etc.), but leave most of the space for ME. I have databases totaling about 25,000 business cards I've collected over the years. These are for personal contacts, IT consultants, potential clients, authors and speakers, services I might buy, etc.

When I come back to the office with a fist full of business cards, they need to be processed. What does that mean? It means that I put them into piles. Some I throw away. Some are very important. Some I promised to send a link or an article. A few I promised an email. Some I want to pitch an idea to. All of the "keepers" are given to an admin to scan into a database.

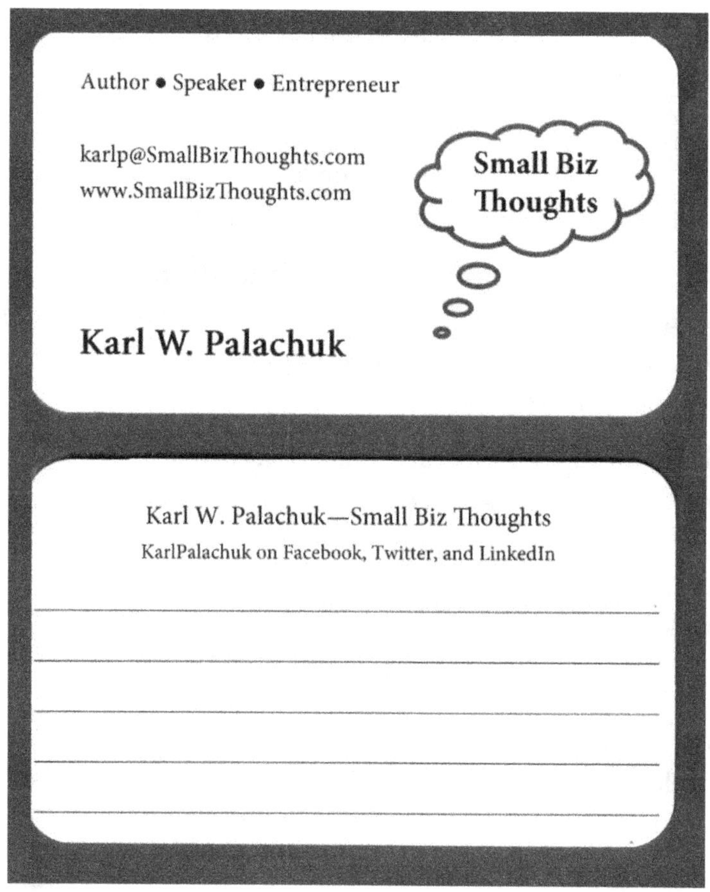

You get the idea.

1) They need to be sorted into appropriate piles

2) Some of them require follow-up

ALL of them need a note about where I met them, the circumstances, and anything interesting about that connection. Where do I write those notes? On The Back of The Business Card!

Oh, but wait. There's crap all over the back of the card. It's dark colored, or has a graph, or a table, it's glossy, or it has a list of useless links. The point is: I can't write on the back of the card if there's no place to write!

Seriously. There are people who collect your business cards and people who don't. The people who don't collect cards don't matter. Period. They will never see the back of your card.

The people who DO collect business cards are pretty consistent in their behavior: They turn it over and write a note about where they met you, when they met you, notes about what they promised you, and other miscellaneous notes.

Now it's up to you: Will you give them a place to write the notes, or will you take it up with self-serving gimmicks that only take up space?

Business Card "Don'ts"

1. Do not print your business card sideways. I believe that 90% of the people who collect business cards will not take you seriously. Some (me included), will simply throw them away.

I guess people think the business card is an opportunity for self-expression, creativity, etc. That's fine. But you don't print your resume or your letterhead in landscape format. Why? Because it's just not done that way. We live in a society where business forms are determined by the norms set down by others.

Your marketing adviser might think that sideways printing makes you stand out and be unique. They're wrong. It's not unique. It's not clever. It's not different enough to make you look like a maverick brainiac. If you want to stand out, change your name to an unpronounceable symbol. But print your business cards like a business professional!

Remember:

There are people who collect your business cards and people who don't. The people who don't collect cards don't matter. The people who collect business cards expect a normal card. Give it to them.

2. Do not use Laser Perf business cards. First, . . . It doesn't matter what's first. Don't do it! Second, let's say you are a professional. Professionals look professional. And they need to look particularly professional with the things that people might associate with your profession.

Computer-printed cards are 99.99% less professional than real business cards. "Free" cards from Vista Print with a logo on the back are better than laser perf. With shipping, Vista Print cards cost about $.04 per card. Laser perf cards are about $.04 per card.

A recent Google search returned "About 274,000,000" hits for Business Cards. And there are more places than that. Staples has in-house printing. 1,000 cards will cost you about $.03 per card - or less. The point is: Laser perf cards are not any cheaper than real, professional cards. AND they look cheap.

And they feel cheap.

If you use high volume, the cards get cheaper and cheaper. 273,999,999 of those online printers will also bargain with you to lower the price more, if you contact them directly or order cards for everyone in the office.

Remember:

There are people who collect your business cards and people who don't. The people who don't collect cards don't matter. The people who collect business cards will make fun of you if you have a laser perf card.

3. Do not have a glossy back on your business cards. See the discussion above. Take it to heart. Most of the time when I am handed a glossy-backed card, I try to write on the back and can't. This does two things. First, it makes you fish around for some other way to give me a writing surface or pen that might work. Second, it totally derails the conversation. Now instead of listening to your elevator speech, we're talking about your stupid business cards.

The lesson: Glossy-backed cards are completely useless. Okay. To be fair, they're useful to people who only scan cards into a database. And completely useless to the other 95% of the people you hand a card to.

I recently was in a conversation where person one was giving a card to person two so he could send something they were talking about. Glossy back. We all brought out pens and pencils to see if anything worked. Finally, I brought out one of my business cards and he wrote the message on that. Then the two cards were folded together so the recipient would remember to send the item to the person whose card was with mine.

Remember:

There are people who collect your business cards and people who don't. The people who don't collect cards don't matter. The people who collect business cards will be really disappointed that you have a glossy card.

4. Do not use reverse print or obnoxious color combinations on your business cards. You've seen it. Dark red background with lime green ink. Your eyes take a minute to focus. Then the type begins to move. Pretty soon you have vertigo. And invariably the business is something like "Creative Solutions."

Really? How about changing your company name to Stupid Decisions or Bad Examples?

Business cards should be functional. Think of the context. You hand your card to someone and they need to quickly get enough information off of it to engage you in a discussion. They might write a note on the back. Then it goes into their pocket until it is processed and scanned.

Unless you actually have black light-enabled cards and hand them out in bars, the reverse printing is just annoying. Our brains don't work like that. Make it readable. Make it useful.

Business Card Dos

Okay, enough complaining. How about a checklist that is useful for constructing and using business cards? Great. Start here.

1. Your Name (you personally) should be clear and visible and readable from arm's length.

That means it is also easy to find. Everyone hates a business card with strange font combinations so you have to scan all over the card to find the person's name. Where's Waldo? Or whoever I'm talking to.

2. Your Company name should be clear and easy to find.

3. Contact information is up to you.

Some cards only have email or only have a phone number. It depends on how you want to be contacted. If you want to give your entire mailing address, fax number, and extension that's fine. Decide WHY you would hand out this information and what you really need on that card to fulfill your needs.

4. Company logo and slogan.

If you have a nice logo or a slogan that really helps you differentiate yourself, then find a place for them on your card. Remember: They should contribute to the goal of making your card useful and easy to use. If they detract, get them out of the way, make them smaller, move them to the side, or drop them altogether.

5. Titles . . . hmmmmm.

Some people need titles. But most of us don't really need titles on our cards. They're just one more thing that needs to be changed if you change jobs. I tend to put titles on my Great Little Book cards. But over at America's Tech Support, Mike prefers no titles.

Does a title do something for you? If yes, put it on the card. If not, leave it off.

I once worked with a client who let everyone pick their own titles. So people had business cards that said "Goddess of the Third Order," "Grand Viseer," etc. It was all fun. Most of these people never met with a client and no one saw their cards except each other. So it was more of a team building exercise than a business decision.

Sometimes we feel obligated to put something on the card for a title. If so, make it descriptive and useful. Or bland and boring. But whatever you do, do it intentionally and not because you feel you need to put something there.

6. Other Information (QR Code, Facebook ID, Fan Pages, LinkedIn, Twitter, Google+, AIM, Pinterest, 4Square, Yelp, Flickr, Reddit, RSS, Technorati, StumbledUpon, Digg, Yahoo Instant Messenger, Jagg, blog, Klout, etc.).

I bet you know where this is going.

There is simply too much miscellaneous stuff to fit it all on a tiny little business card. So if you want to put something else on there, be picky. Choose a few things that don't take up much space AND that contribute to your marketing goals.

7. Use the back Wisely. Or leave it blank.

Remember, the back of the card is not for ten little tips, quotations, IP Subnet calculators, etc. The back is primarily for notes. You can use some of the back for links, logos, QR code, etc. But leave at least half of it blank - or lined for notes.

8. Make your business card scan-able. You should have a business card scanner. If not, visit your more successful competition and borrow theirs. Make sure that your business card is clean and clear enough that it scans well.

This little tip will go a long way to making sure you've addressed several of the points in this article. The fonts and colors won't be crazy. The text is actually legible. The card is printed correctly (not sideways). And so forth.

The Strategic Use of Business Cards

Step back a minute and ask yourself: WHY do you have business cards? What will you do with them? How do you expect others to use them? What role do they play in your business? Here are two examples.

At our MSP, we hand out business cards very freely to anyone who might be a potential client, partner, or be able to connect us with a potential client or partner. The office manager hardly ever uses them. The techs rarely use them. The owner and service manager are the primary users/distributors. These cards have full contact information because they appeal to a local audience (address, phone, email, etc.).

At Great Little Book / Small Biz Thoughts, I have several brands and some of them have business cards. My cards are intended to give someone a means to contact me. I mostly use them at conferences so that people have my email address and web site. No matter which web site they start at, my goal is to eventually get them to add themselves to my mailing list.

The card I hand out the most (Small Biz Thoughts) does not have a phone number. I don't want people to be irritated if they don't know that I never answer my phone. So it's email and web site. The other card is for authors and speakers, and people who might potentially hire me to speak. This card does have the phone number. These people still use voicemail as a primary means of communication. I still don't answer the phone, but they have a place to call. These cards have no address information. It's irrelevant for them.

You have to figure out why you need business cards, what role they plan in your business, and therefore what they should contain. And to be honest, if you hardly ever hand them out, the more basic the better. Don't spend a fortune with cards that no one will see.

Here's one big tip about business cards: Don't act like they cost $1 each! They are the cheapest advertising you can buy. At my MSP, we buy ours 100 or 250 at a time. For Great Little Book, I buy them 1,000 at a time. I am the Johnny Appleseed of business cards - scattering them everywhere I go.

How To Buy Business Cards

If your local printer can compete with online digital printers, great. If not, go find an online place you like. I've had both good and bad experiences with Vista Print (www.vistaprint.com). I have to say that their cards are first rate with regard to paper. And I like the default "flat" finish. It can be hard to get printers to understand that you want a glossy front and a flat back.

I have used OvernightPrints.com (www.overnightprints.com) several times and been very pleased. Even if they do something wrong, they fix it no questions asked and super fast. They have a variety of downloadable templates (MS Word, Adobe Illustrator, etc.). I also like uprinting.com (www.uprinting.com) because they do a nice job with rounded corners and interesting die cuts. Just make sure you pick a shape that will successfully go through a business card scanner!

If you are not proficient enough to use Publisher, Illustrator, or some other program to design business cards, please hire someone who is. Odesk.com, Elance.com, 99designs.com, and a million other places can get this done for cheap. You might even hire an intern from the local design school for $10/hr. It's more than they would make working for McDonald's, and it builds their portfolio.

Many sites (most sites?) have wizards so you can create your cards online. Click-click-click and you're done. Upload your logo and away you go. Generally speaking, if you produce your own design, you will upload it as a PDF file. Be sure to embed the fonts so it doesn't get kicked back to you.

Organize Your Business Cards

I know this will shock you if you're a regular reader, but we have a standard location for all business cards and related files. On our primary drive, it's under \Marketing\Business Cards. That's where we keep copies of the source files, source graphics, QR codes, etc. Illustrator and PDF files are named after the person with a date embedded in the name. e.g., "Biz_Card_KarlP_20141130.pdf" We use the underscore in case spaces cause a problem with the machine we're uploading to.

Keeping all your cards in one place makes it easy to create new cards that are completely consistent with everyone else in the company. It also makes it easy to change formats for all cards if you make a company-wide change. If you have a generational change like that, you should put the old format into a sub-directory.

Three Take-Aways from This Chapter:

1. Most business cards are horrible and poorly designed. Don't let yours be like that.
2. Be very intentional about the contents and design of your business cards. Make them usable.
3. Have your business cards professionally printed with a flat back so people can write notes there.

Three Action Steps for Your Company:

1. ______________________________

   ____

2. ______________________________

   ____

3. ______________________________

   ____

36

Quarterly Roadmap Meetings

There are a handful of things we do that truly define our business and separate us from other IT providers. One is our monthly maintenance process (see volume four in this series). Another is our Quarterly Roadmap Meetings.

Roadmap meetings actually start with prospects before they become clients. Many of the questions are the same. Basically, you want to get a sense where the client's business is today and where they expect to be in the next year or so. If you can, you should try to find out where they hope to be in five years.

Basically, the Roadmap is a rough plan for the client's technology "department" (even though most do not have such a department). The Roadmap meeting is an opportunity to sit down with the client and talk about their future.

Three Benefits of Quarterly Roadmap Meetings

First: We use our Roadmap questionnaire to get to know clients and help assess their technology. In my opinion, this is far superior to an assessment of technology alone. Once we know what the company wants to do, we can determine whether they have the right technology now, and what they will need in the future.

Second: For existing clients, these regular meetings provide a non-sales discussion of their technology so we can really participate as a member of their team. This helps us stay connected to the client on a casual level when we're not addressing a service request.

Third: As the clients plan their technology spending, we can plan our sales. It's very nice to know when projects are coming up and when we will be selling servers, workstations, etc.

What We Talk About

Is the client growing or shrinking? How dependent are they on technology? Do they have a budget? Do they have a *technology* budget? It is quite amazing how easy it is to get clients to tell you their plans, hopes, and dreams. We've gotten responses like these:

"We're having financial problems and need to cut back."

"We're going to add three more people this year."

"We have $3 Million in revenue and expect it to be $3.5M within 18 months."

This is great stuff. You only get this stuff by asking.

But you can't casually ask. You need to have a process and procedure in which 1) They've agreed to participate, and 2) These are just a few questions in a longer list.

We use our own "Roadmap" process, but many of the questions are similar to the original Microsoft Business and Technology

Assessment Toolkit. The best place to get this is from an old MSDN or Technet CD from at least five years ago. That's because the assessment was just a Word document and was easy to customize.

To my knowledge, there is no current version or this questionnaire at Microsoft. The last version they produced required InfoPath, a program they have ceased to produce. Note that this is not the same as the Microsoft Assessment and Planning Toolkit, which is for evaluating client technology so you can give advice on upgrades and migrations.

Our Roadmap Questionnaire is included with the download materials for this book.

We print out our questions on blue paper with a cover sheet so it looks like a set of forms. That way prospects and clients see that there really is a standardized process here.

When clients are growing, you can give them the big heads up that technology spending will increase. No "sales" necessary. Just say things like "You know you can't add three people and all their data in that old server. So you don't need a new server today, but you know you will."

There's no sales here, so they'll just nod their head and say "I know, I know."

But not everyone is growing. In the recent recession we have had to help several clients manage the shrinking of their business. That includes using the best machines as some machines are taken out of service. In two cases it meant helping the clients shut down their physical office and move to virtual offices (and to the cloud). In one case, we managed technology as our client was purchased by their competition.

Our company provides free planning meetings for our clients under contract. Our definition of "managed services" focuses heavily on being the outsourced I.T. department for our clients. As such, we try to help develop the budget, the policies, and the 1-year, 3-year, and 5-year plans for the "I.T. Department." Basically, if they have a big business plan or binder, we provide the I.T. section that slips into place.

Here are some examples of activities we promote through Roadmap meetings:

- Some clients buy whatever brand of computers and equipment is the cheapest. We help them see the longer-term savings of standardization for PCs, monitors, UPSs, etc. This is a gradual change over time.

- For some clients, open licenses make the most sense. For many small businesses, OEM licenses make more sense. We help clients gradually move to the right licensing programs as technology refreshes.
- Clients always have concerns about upgrades - servers and workstations. So again we help them create a plan so that decisions are mostly made when a machine needs to be ordered.

As you can see, all of these decisions are interrelated. And they all involve lots of money and labor. And timing matters. MOST small businesses make these decisions one at a time, trying to save the most money on each purchase. The result is that they spend more money as time goes on.

And we don't push upgrades just to push upgrades. If Microsoft gave these folks everything they wanted for free, they would still have the costs of our labor plus downtime per desktop and potential downtime for servers just to install it all. So we don't push every update that comes down the road.

Scheduling Meetings

We call these "Quarterly" Roadmap Meetings. But that almost never happens. Basically, we schedule them with all clients. Our office manager knows that Mike and I have certain slots open in our calendar, so she can fill those with Roadmap meetings and knows they won't conflict with anything else. It also means that we spread out the meetings so we're not taken off of tech support or other tasks for large chunks of the week.

Once we've completed a round of Roadmap Meetings, she starts scheduling them again. Some clients delay and delay. So overall, most clients end up having 1-3 meetings a year. But that's enough. It keeps us in touch and keeps the conversation going.

Meetings are generally one or two hours. This is not a time to address individual service ticket issues, but it IS a time to discuss service overall. If clients have concerns about nagging issues or overall service, this is a great opportunity for them to bring that up.

Three Take-Aways from This Chapter:

1. Schedule "Roadmap" meetings with every client. You'll be amazed at how good this is for business.
2. Customize forms for your business and use them consistently.
3. Roadmap meetings cannot be sales meetings. At the same time, you'll always get sales out of the meetings.

Three Action Steps for Your Company:

1. ______________________________

____

2. ______________________________

____

3. ______________________________

____

37

Helping Clients with Audits - Security and Insurance

Several years ago, our largest client was a company that works with extremely secure information for Fortune 100 companies. The kind of information that makes the news when it gets leaked. So, obviously, the information must be secured.

From the beginning, these folks needed very high standards on email security, web site security, database security, and all the network security stuff we were used to dealing with. Please note that Manuel (president of my company at the time) had worked in I.T. at Bonneville Power Administration. Think nuclear power. I was once the Site Manager for PC Software Support at HP's Roseville plant.

We were not strangers to security or audits.

But this client brought us some serious challenges.

This client was constantly responding to security audit requests. As a result, they turned to us. Very often, they would forward to us a 200 page questionnaire about network security. Most of it was pretty mundane (e.g., encryption level of SSL certs and when they expire). But some stuff was pretty interesting.

For example:

Dual Firewalls

One insurance company wanted two firewalls configured as in the illustration in order to limit access to their data from outside the company LAN. They did not trust using a VLAN on the same firewall that touched the Internet. Luckily for us, these were nice, high-end, expensive firewalls.

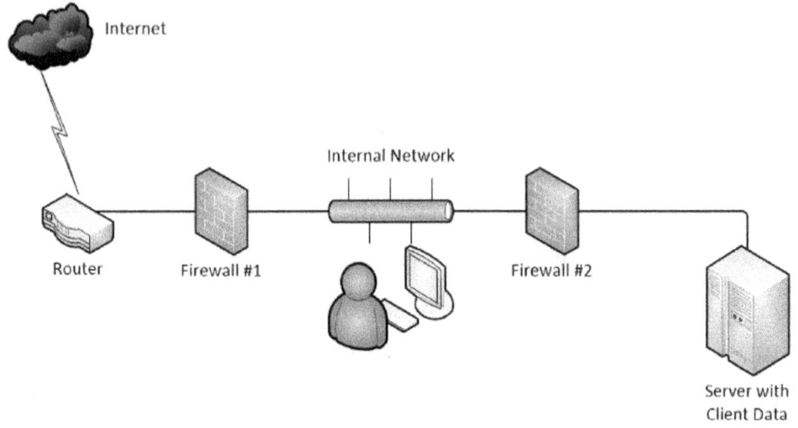

VPN to MSP

One company (our client's client) required a hardware VPN between the client and us so that all traffic, including RMM agent, moved between us on a secure line.

Roof Access

One company required that access from the roof of the commercial building be padlocked and monitored via alarm company. This is so someone cannot be lowered to the roof via helicopter and gain access to the building.

Building-Wide Facilities

One company required that facilities (electrical closet, Internet access panels, etc.) be monitored by the alarm company.

Encryption

One company asked that data be encrypted while at rest on the client folders or database. So, data arrived encrypted, needed to be decrypted to import to database, then re-encrypted. Once client data has been imported into the database, the source data must be encrypted.

Programmer Access

One insurance company required that the programmer have access to the code only and should be restricted from viewing any of the client data. The client lead programmer had access to all software databases. This cannot be changed without a significant change in processes. The programmer was made a full time member of client's staff, passed a security check, and signed all non-disclosure agreements.

Independent Audits

One company required that an independent third party (other than us) perform a network security audit of the processes and documentation implemented by us.

The first time we went through one of these audits, I think it took about four hours to cover the basics and two hours to take care of some of the esoteric stuff. Then we had some documentation and remediation to do. Followed by meetings and meetings. All billable. It was easily 25 hours total at full price.

The second time we went through an audit, we had most of the answers already in some form. We mostly copied and pasted from the earlier audit. I don't recall exactly, but maybe a couple hours for the audit and report, plus a few hours for remediation, and a few hours for meetings.

After that, we rarely had remediation and we could pump out the audit and report in two hours flat (plus any meetings that we requested).

Who Requests An Audit?

Every industry is different. But secure data has some common characteristics across industries. See the diagram on "Who Requests an Audit?" Most audits are requested directly by our client's client. Sometimes it's that end-client's insurance company that needs the audit.

Second, in our experience, is our client's insurance company. This is normally their Liability company, but it might also be Errors & Omissions. Knowing that the client is subject to a variety of regulations and has liabilities regarding the protection of end-client data, the insurance companies want to minimize their risk.

Third, there are government agencies. This is more of a threat than an ongoing activity. While our client was subject to certain government regulations (and feared an audit), they were never actually audited by a government agency.

With some industries, government audits or reports are much more regular. More and more, financial and medical businesses are under increased government regulation. It's actually a pretty good idea to consider creating a niche in one of these industries.

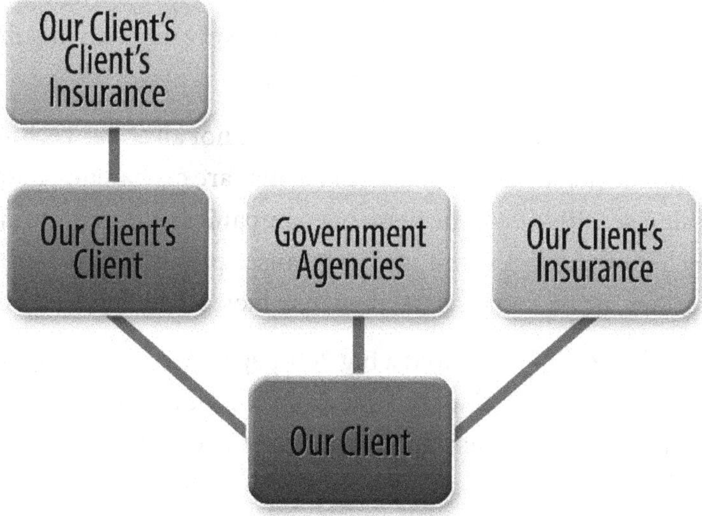

The Forms

I wish I could give you a form, or list of questions. But the only examples I have are from HUGE companies with massive legal departments willing to enforce their non-disclosure agreements very strongly.

(Having said that, I have a project on the back burner to find a way to obtain and release this information without tying it to a specific company.)

One great place to start looking at the kinds of questions you'll find in a big-company audit is on ITSecurity.com's web site (see http://www.itsecurity.com/features/it-security-audit-010407/). When you look at their list of items to be aware of, just turn every tiny thing into a question. Then consider how you would answer it.

As a general rule, there are a LOT more regulations and security audits for companies with fifty or more employees. And, again, there are a lot more audits for companies that are working with or sub-contracting for major corporations.

Fortune 100 and Fortune 500 companies are not all alike. Technology audits are most common for companies that are exchanging data or processing sensitive data for these big companies. For example, if you have a client that works with medical transcriptions, credit card applications, or personnel data, they may have a few "big fish" clients.

Once you have either acquired a big 200-page form or figured out what you think a number of the questions are, you can begin offering an auditing service to your largest clients. OR you can pay some money for the exam prep and get certified in CISSP, CAP, SSCP, or CSSLP by starting at https://www.isc2.org. See Appendix A for definitions of the alphabet soup.

That training includes 98% of what you need to provide all the audits your clients could ever want.

The Business Model

A few notes about going into the "auditing" business.

First, it is really easy. I'm sorry for all the folks selling certs, but it's not difficult. It's just tedious and you have to be extremely precise. But most of the questions are along the lines of "Is there a backup plan? Describe it in detail." So if you're addicted to documentation, you're good to go.

Second, the key clients for this are 50+ employees serving at least a few Fortune 500 companies. This is just a great combo of needs and resources. These folks see the audit as "time off task" and a pain in the neck. The result: They are willing to simply pay money to make the problem go away.

Third, once you do one super-monster audit, you'll have almost all the verbiage to complete the next one. If you're been doing your job, then there is a documented process for passwords, backups, remote access, encryption, file storage, etc. Writing all that out in detail will help you to create even better documentation for all of your clients!

Fourth, if you decide to add professional security audits to your portfolio, you'll need to do a lot more than "get by" with an audit or two. This world changes fast, so you'll need to commit to perpetual education. But if you do that, you will have very little competition. Unless you live in one of the top ten metropolitan areas of the U.S., you might find that only one or two people in your area have the training to perform such audits. That makes it a great niche.

Fifth, this business really is perpetual. Most clients who need a high-level audit also need one or two additional audits. And they need these repeated on some schedule (annual, biennial, etc.). Not only that, but clients talk to other people in their field. So if you're "the" place to get a great audit, then you get a referral. And an audit within the same field is even easier the second time!

SOP - Standard Operating Procedure

Unlike general technology consulting, security auditing is a pretty well defined area. In general consulting, you are likely to stumble on almost any technical issue out there. But with security audits, there really is a limited field. The questionnaire might be 200 pages, but 195 of those pages will be the same from client to client.

The first key to success in this field is to go get your clients. That is, you need to figure out who needs an audit and make sure they know you exist. They might not have a request from Exxon, Walmart, or GE on their desk. But if they expect to see one in the next 12 months, they will keep your information and call you when they need you.

Niche, niche, niche.

The second key to success is to continually improve your "verbiage" for answering the questions. The goal for you is to help your client pass the audit. So you need to find the right words that make it look like they are absolutely above reproach. Once you have the golden words, save them for the next audit.

Of course, you need to be brutally honest if the client needs to make improvements. And, with luck, you'll get some work out of that. But even with areas of improvement, you can save the good descriptions for use on the next audit.

The third key to success is that you probably need to do these yourself. Or maybe you have one superstar tech who can do audits. But you CANNOT just hand this off to an entry level technician. So audits need to be done by the senior techs.

In the end, doing security audits is just another niche. And the better you are at your niche, the fewer competitors you have. And, the better you are, the more you can charge!

If you decide this niche is for you, it might be useful to build a keyword-based database or spreadsheet so you can find and re-use verbiage as needed. Again, you need to customize each response. But there's no point in starting over from scratch.

Three Take-Aways from This Chapter:

1. Security Auditing is a great niche – One in which clients are guaranteed to have the budget needed.
2. Start with one and work hard on the answers. Save those answers for future audits.
3. Most audit questions are the same, but you have to stay on your toes because technology changes all the time.

Three Action Steps for Your Company:

1. ____

   ____

2. ____

   ____

3. ____

   ____

38

Celebrate Anniversaries and Birthdays

If nothing else, small business is a world of personal connections. Unlike mega-corps, there are few employees, few owners, and few clients. So it makes a difference when you pay attention to the little things.

One of my favorite features on Facebook is the birthday list. I like to see who has a birthday today and send a quick note. Not to total strangers (since I have about 5,000 connections, many are strangers), but to people I know or have done business with.

Celebrate Client Anniversaries

Early on, our company started sending birthday greetings if we know a client's birthday. Not generic corporate cards, but just fun birthday cards I bought at the store. After all, we didn't really know that many birthdays.

More importantly, we started celebrating major client anniversaries. These started at the one year mark. I bought a small gift, like a bottle of wine, and presented the client with a card and the gift. I always keep my eye out for good gifts. One time I gave a client a 25 pound Hershey's chocolate bar. It was big and fun.

For five and ten year anniversaries I step it up quite a bit, especially for larger clients. I throw an actual party with a cake and punch.

Many bakeries can print a "photo" onto a sheet cake. We order up a cake with a picture of us and the client, or with our logos together and a message that says "Thank you for five great years."

Some bakeries are really sticklers about logos, fearing copyright infringement. I think they had one warning about copy rights and trademarks and they're scared to death . . . even though they display large knock-off images of Disney characters. Anyway, some won't put your logo on the cake . . . not even your own logo. Find another bakery or settle for a nice font.

The key point is to actually celebrate your business partnership.

Remember, most businesses aren't IN business for five years, let alone having a five year anniversary of doing business with another company. And ten years is very rare stuff.

Celebrate Employee Birthdays

This is very simple. You might go to lunch or just buy a cake and sing Happy Birthday at the office.

As adults we rarely celebrate birthdays in a major way unless they end with a 5 or 0. So it's nice when people in the office bring out a cake and a card that everyone signed.

It's also nice to give your team a half hour of hanging out with each other and chatting casually instead of only working together.

If you have a larger staff, you may want to combine the January birthdays, February birthdays, etc. If you can spring for a give card to Best Buy or some other place, that's always appreciated.

Implementation is Easy

Someone (office manager?) needs to keep track of employee birthdays. Just keep a list, and keep it updated when you hire someone.

The same goes for clients: Create a schedule that includes the first month they were ever billed for services. This is very easy to figure out. Just open QuickBooks and look at the details for that client. Go back to the first entry. It will be an invoice for the first job you did.

If you would rather track the first time they signed a managed service contract, that may take a little more work. But all the answers are in QuickBooks.

We used Send Out Cards (https://www.sendoutcards.com/) for a long time. But you can also simply buy cards for your clients. The volume is low since you'll rarely have more than four or five anniversaries in a month. And you only go all-out on biggies.

The bottom line is that implementing a party policy is easy. You just have to decide to do it.

. . . And remember that it's the little things that matter in the long run.

Three Take-Aways from This Chapter:

1. Celebrate birthdays if you can. Definitely celebrate client anniversaries. Make them feel loved.
2. Get a customized cake with your logo and the client's logo.
3. Invite all of your staff and all of the client's staff so they can hang out without "technology" being part of the party.

Three Action Steps for Your Company:

1. ____

2. ____

3. ____

39

Sales Tickets and Sales Queues

This post assumes you have a ticketing system of time kind. You may or may not have a CRM (customer relationship management) system, or a PSA (professional services automation) with CRM built in. But you do have a ticketing system.

Many people use QuoteWerks (www.quotewerks.com) or Quosal (www.quosal.com) or some other tool for getting out quotes. Some people use the CRM module of their PSA. Some use Salesforce.com or another stand-alone CRM system. But many small shops don't do enough quotes to justify buying or investing time into these tools.

This article gives some tips on managing the internal communication around sales within your ticketing system. Our primary goal here is to make sure nothing gets lost, dropped, or forgotten. Our secondary goal is to smooth out asynchronous communications between sales staff, sales engineers, front office, and technicians.

First: Sales Queue/Sales Board

Depending on your PSA or ticketing system, you should either have a queue or a board devoted to sales. Sales means everything from RFQ (request for quote) to quote, negotiation, sale, payment, or ordering the hardware and software. In other words, it's everything that happens right up to the point where an actual service request is created so technicians can go do the work.

Whether you have a sales person or do it all yourself, it's a good habit to have sales activity take place in the sales queue. That way the sales person doesn't lose anything and the technicians don't have to worry about it until they need to do something.

Second: The Flow of the Sales Process

As you define statuses that make sense for your organization, it is helpful to plot out how a prospective sale flows through your ticketing system. Here is a typical flow:

- Client requests a quote for a new desktop.
    - Technician acknowledges the service request. The ticket is placed in the Sales Queue, assigned to the sales person, and the status is changed to "Sales."
- The sales person generates a quote and sends it to the client.
    - The ticket status is changed to "Waiting on Client."
- The client asks for options regarding hard drive size. The sales person changes the status to "Sales" unless he is able to turn around a revised quote in short order. In either case, the status goes to "Waiting on Client" after the revised quote is produced.
- The client approves the quote.
    - The Sales person generates an invoice and puts a note in the system about what is coming.
    - The Sales person EITHER moves this quote to the appropriate service queue or creates new tickets in the

appropriate tech support queue. In either case, the ticket status is now "Waiting on Client."

- Client payment is processed.
  - The front office puts a note in the ticket that payment has been received.
  - Assuming the sales person does the ordering, the status is changed to "Sales."
- Equipment and software are ordered.
  - The ticket status is changed to "Waiting on Parts."
- Equipment and software arrive.
  - The ticket status is changed to "Schedule This."

Note: At this point the sales person is out of the picture, the front office staff are out of the picture, and the service ticket is now in the appropriate service queue.

Note that this flow allows all departments to "communicate" with each other through the ticketing system. At no point are two departments required to sit down and talk through all this face to face. If they get a chance (and that's very likely), great. But nothing in this process allows the flow to get stuck just because two people couldn't be in the same office at the same time.

At the end of this flow, the ticket is no longer in the sales queue but in a support queue (e.g., Level I). And the status is Schedule This, so the service manager knows it is ready to work on.

Migrations and Complicated Tickets

In more complex cases, a sales process might result in a series of service tickets. In this case you will definitely not covert one sales ticket into a single service ticket. For example, our migration process (see *The Network Migration Workbook*) results in seven distinct service requests. Even a simple new office installation might result in tickets for

- Firewall configuration
- Server Build
- Server Setup
- Data Migration
- Workstation Build
- Workstation Delivery
- Printer Setup
- Testing, Documentation, Fine-Tuning

The never-ever-ever-ending rule is that you cannot lose anything or "drop" anything. The system you design must work so that everything in the quote is entered into the system as some kind of action (order the right equipment, set it up, train the users, etc.). And the minute all items are ready for action, the status will reflect that to the tech department.

If you do have some kind of quoting module in your PSA or CRM system, I encourage you to learn that and see how well it works for you. Many of these systems have no way to convert CRM/quoting activity into service tickets. But some do, so explore that option.

Whether you implement a sales flow similar to this in your ticketing system or not, you really need to have some kind of sales flow. It should allow you to make sure quotes (and pieces of quotes) don't get lost. It should also facilitate communication between the departments. Start by literally drawing out this flow on a piece of paper. Then create a Visio or other diagram so that you can visualize the flow. Finally, create the processes within your ticketing system to make this happen.

And of course you have to document your process.

Three Take-Aways from This Chapter:

1. Draw a diagram of how sales flow through your company. Write out a process for that.
2. In your sales process, every deliverable or action must result in a ticket or status in your system.
3. Do not let sales slow down or stall because two people don't get a chance to sit down and talk about it.

Three Action Steps for Your Company:

1. ______________________________

____

2. ______________________________

____

3. ______________________________

____

40

Trip Charges and On Site Minimums

One area of service delivery has changed dramatically over the last five years: On Site vs. Remote support. We rarely go on site to clients for support these days. Almost every on site visit is related to sales or client relations. Some of us have clients in other states and other countries.

The really good news about remote support is that it's a lot more profitable, particularly if you have employees. Let's use the example of a client that's 20 miles from your office and it takes about 30 minutes to drive there and park. So an on-site visit takes about one hour longer than the time you are actually on site.

If you pay an employee to make that visit, you (should) pay 56.5 cents per mile for the mileage reimbursement. So that's $22.60. And let's say your tech earns $20/hr so your real cost is about $25 just for the travel time. At this point you are out $47.60 just to BE on site. If you have to pay for parking, it's easily more than $50. A senior engineer might be twice that.

Note: Even if it's you and not an employee, you need to make the same calculation. This is critical to understanding your cost of delivering service!

Do You Charge for Trips?

You have two basic options for recouping these costs: Charge a "trip charge" or charge a minimum that guarantees you will be profitable.

Most MSPs have a minimum charge rather than a trip charge. For whatever reason, there is some resistance to a charge just for showing up. Having said that, every consultant I've talked to who **does** have a trip charge says they have no problems with it. They just make it part of their policies and clients know it's coming. So it becomes a non-issue.

Luckily, in our business, a one hour minimum is normally enough to guarantee that we're profitable. If the travel to and from a client's office costs you about $50, and the next hour on site costs another $25, then you are making some profit as long as your hourly rate is $76 or more.

Of course you don't want a profit of only $1 for two hours of your employee's time. At $100/hr you will make at least $25.

To make the on-site minimum work, you need to make sure that you keep travel time within the 30 minute drive time. One cool way to do this is with Microsoft MapPoint. See the graphic.

First you plot your office. Then choose the option to define a drive time zone of 30 minutes. MapPoint will draw the zone automatically. From there you can make a few adjustments. But it's a great start on determining your "One Hour Minimum" drive zone.

If you're a Microsoft Certified Partner or a MAPs ("Action Pack") subscriber, then you have access to MapPoint. See http://www.microsoft.com/partner. If you haven't played with it, this is a great place to start.

Microsoft MapPoint Driving Zone

When you write your policy about "local" travel, this is your local travel area. Within this area you should find most of your clients. Within the zone (your local area), there is a one-hour minimum.

Outside this area you need a higher minimum. It might be three hours or four hours. It depends on the distance. In Sacramento, we have a nice compact area around the metro area. But we have a lot of clients in the Bay Area - a minimum of 1.5 hours drive each way with perfect traffic. So those clients have a four hour minimum. On average, 3-4 hours is needed just for travel. So even an hour on site costs us a lot of money.

Here's the basic outline for your SOP:

1. Do you have a separate Trip Charge? Yes/No
2. If no, what is your on-site minimum for local travel?
3. Is there a second "zone" for travel (e.g., 31-60 minutes of travel time)?
4. If not, how do you calculate on-site minimums for non-local travel?

Train Your Employees To Stay Profitable

It is very important that your employees understand the cost of travel time. There are hard costs (e.g., the $50 calculated above) and there are opportunity costs. If you pay someone to drive two hours a day and do not charge for that, you have lost the opportunity to have that person bill out two hours of labor for remote support.

Encourage technicians to group their travel in order to minimize it. For example, combine client visits so that you don't have a trip all the way back to the office between clients.

Discourage on site visits for tech support unless they are really necessary. We can close more tickets and bill more hours if we work remotely.

Control travel in general. Your employees should not be "running errands" like driving to the store to get a network cable. Plan your day. Have enough supplies on hand so that such trips are unnecessary.

This is the kind of policy that might seem trivial, but it can have a significant effect on your profitability – even if you are a one-person shop. Time spent driving is always less profitable than time spent working. And with remote support being so widely available, there are fewer and fewer tasks that have to be done on site.

Three Take-Aways from This Chapter:

1. Travel time is always less profitable that work time.
2. Set a "30 minute" travel zone around your office and focus your clients inside this area.
3. Determine profitable minimum hourly charges for 1-30 minute travel and 31-60 minute travel.

Three Action Steps for Your Company:

1. ____

2. ____

3. ____

41

Sales Scripts

There are many, many ways to approach sales. Different approaches work with different prospects, different products, and at different times. It's hard to say which approach is the best for a given circumstance. But it's easy to say which is the worst: A totally random, off the top of your head, impromptu rambling.

Some time ago I wrote a blog post on "The Worst Sales Call Ever." (Go to http://blog.smallbizthoughts.com/2008/10/worst-sales-call-ever.html or just go to blog.smallbizthoughts.com and search for "The Worst Sales Call Ever.") One of the messages in that post is that **any sales call is better than no sales call**. Having said that, the more systemic your approach, the more successful you will be.

If you have a process, you can measure the results and fine-tune the process. If everything is random then improvement is also random. It will come and it will go, but you will have no effect on it one way or the other.

Note: Sales is different from Marketing. They are obviously related. Marketing pushes prospects closer and closer to the sale. Sales take place when you ask people to give you their money. So the sales script is not part of marketing. It is a standardized process for asking people to give you their money.

As a Standard Operating Procedure, it's a good idea to create a sample sales script that you can tweak and tune for each new campaign. Use it for servers this quarter and BDRs next quarter.

Writing A Sales Script

The first step in writing a sales script is to figure out the classic Five W's: Who, What, Why, When, and Where. Start by creating a form with five questions and write a bit about each.

Who are you selling to? Existing clients, new prospects, big companies, small companies, lawyers, accountants, etc.

What are you selling? Is this campaign for hosted services, BDRs, managed service contracts, or something else?

Why should the prospect buy? Remember: Focus on solving a problem, not listing features. Clients don't care about megahertz and gigabits.

When do you need the sale? Is this offer good until the end of the month? 90 days? This adds an element of scarcity, which is an important piece of the sales process.

Where (in this context) is about the context of the sales script. Will it be by phone, in a formal presentation, or in a face to face meeting?

Once you know the Five W's, you can start to write the script. Now that you have put down in words what you're selling, who you're selling it to, etc. it will be a lot easier.

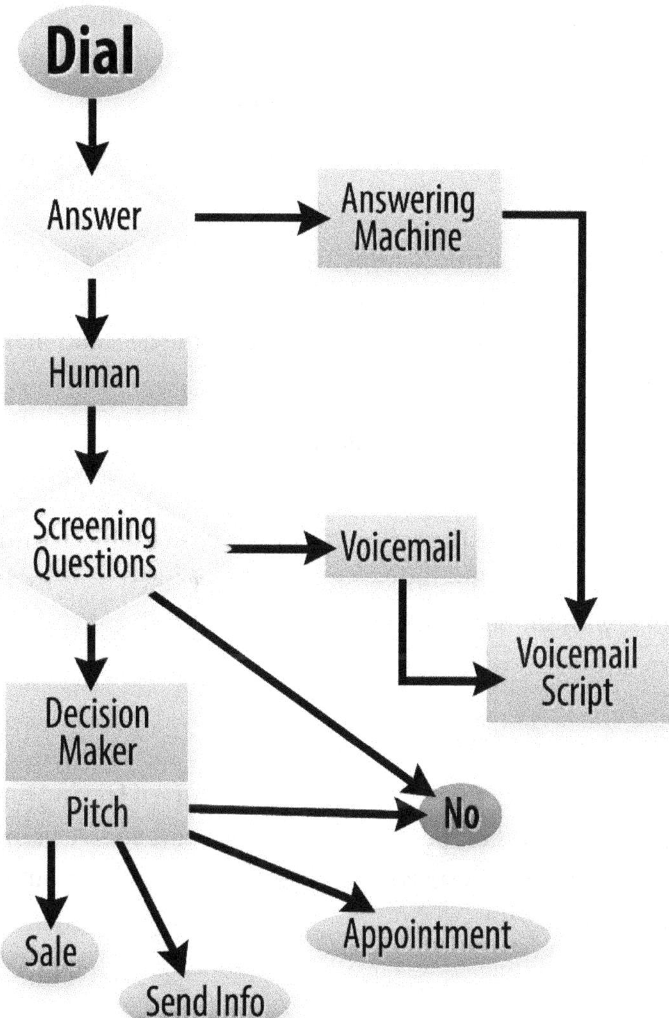

Sales Call Flow

Keep It Simple

Take a look at the flow chart. Most calls go more or less like this. Of course you need to fill in the details. But just look at the flow and write down what you'll say at each point. Essentially, you'll need three mini-scripts, only one of which is the sales pitch.

First, you need a script for when you hit voicemail, which you use most.

Second, you need a script for when a human answers. Your goal is to get them to not hang up – and then pass you to someone who can give you money. Or maybe you get passed to the decision maker's voicemail.

Third, you need a script for the decision maker. This, at last, is your pitch!

The simpler you make the script, the easier it is to deliver without being nervous. Plus, the simpler it is, the more likely you are to get through it without being interrupted with a "No Thanks."

Practice Makes Perfect

Now, you make your first call. As you find yourself leaving one voicemail after another, be sure to take notes and update your script as needed. When you hear yourself speaking the words, you might want to tweak and fine-tune.

And when you finally get to talk to the gatekeeper, you'll fine-tune that script.

And the same goes for the decision maker. This is the most important script. So you'll want to fine tune it a lot. Take particular note of things you say that lead to a "yes" - whether it's yes to a sale or yes to an appointment.

A Simple Script to Get You Started

Script One: Voice Mail

> "Hi. This is Karl from KPEnterprises. Phone number 916-555-1212. I'm calling today to see if you would like to have a conversation about your technology and how we can improve your business with Cloud Services. Please give me a call at 916-555-1212. Thank you for your time."

or

> "Hi! This is Karl Palachuk from KPEnterprises. I'm hoping you can return my call at 916-555-1212. We're offering a free 30-minute educational program called "5 Ways Cloud Computing Can Help Your Business Spend Less Every Month." It's about how cloud computing is helping companies like yours improve office efficiency and cut technology costs by as much as 30%. I'd love to give you some more information, so please give me a call when you can. Again, this is Karl from KPEnterprises and you can reach me at 916-555-1212."

Script Two: Gatekeeper

> "Hi. This is Karl with KPEnterprises. I'm trying to reach Mr./Ms. __________ to offer a free educational presentation about how cloud computing is saving companies like yours as much as 30% on their annual technology budget. The presentation takes about 30 minutes, and I've got some openings next week. Do you think that's something he/she would like to hear about?"

Script Three: The Decision Maker

> "Hi! This is Karl with KPEnterprises.
>
> I'm calling today because we've put together an educational program for local businesses called "5 Ways Cloud Computing Can Help Your Business Spend Less Every Month." It's all about how the latest cloud computing technologies are helping companies cut their technology budgets by up to 30%. Are you familiar with cloud technology?"

Yes or No, doesn't matter.

> "Great! They've given me the job of getting these presentations scheduled for local businesses, and I'm calling to see when we might be able to come out and show you the program. It takes about 30 minutes. Of course we're selling something, but the program is full of great information for your business. Do you have 30 minutes available next week?"

IF No:

> "OK. At the very least, can I send you some information about this by email? Would that be alright with you? Great! What's your email address?"

If Yes:

> "Great! Would you be available for an appointment next Tuesday at 10:00?"

If decision maker says they have an in-house IT person:

> "Yes, of course, and I think it would be a great idea for your internal IT staff to be included in the presentation. I've got some openings next week; would you both be available Tuesday at 10:00?"

Of all of these, you'll give the voicemail speech more than anything else. That's good. You'll get very good at it. Notice that you give your phone number twice – and very clearly. There's nothing worse than listening to a voicemail five times to figure out the phone number.

The bottom line on sales scripts: Any script is better than no script. A script will help you be less nervous. You'll sound more natural every time you deliver it.

… And you'll make more sales!

Three Take-Aways from This Chapter:

1. Any sales script is better than no script.
2. Be prepared to leave a lot of voicemails. Be clear and brief.
3. Sales is still a numbers game, so expect more people to so No than Yes. But never take it personally. Just dial the next number.

Three Action Steps for Your Company:

1. ______________________________

   ____

2. ______________________________

   ____

3. ______________________________

   ____

42

Clients Who Abuse the Phones

The client's always right, right? In a word, NO! For the most part, I'm a big fan of the concept that the client is always right. But there are times when the client is just plain wrong. One example of that is when they abuse your phones.

We've already covered basic Phone Etiquette and Procedures in Chapters Twelve and Thirteen. This is more of a policy discussion.

Phone habits with clients are a very simple communication system with two components: You and Your Client. You each play a role in the behavior of the other.

Most clients only work during the work day, with few exceptions. Some clients work "all the time" and call whenever they feel like it. Most of the businesses they work with don't answer the phones after hours, so they're used to just leaving a message and getting a response in the morning. The same goes for weekends.

If by some chance you answer the phone, then the client knows that you're available evenings and weekends. And you might be. If you don't want to be available then, you need to practice the words "Just because you're reached me doesn't mean that I'm available."

It is much better to set policies about when you're available and spell them out on your voicemail message. Once you set your policies, it is very acceptable to expect clients to honor them. Luckily, 99% of all clients are professional and understand that people have normal lives. (Please remember that: Everything that follows is for a very tiny percent of all clients you'll have.)

So what constitutes abuse of the phones? There are three basic types of abuse:

1. Calling every possible extension and phone number in order to create a sense of urgency.
2. Use telephones to interrupt your work and push themselves to the top of your agenda, without regard to your processes.
3. Actual verbal abuse - or insulting - of your employees.

Number Three is the easiest abuse to deal with. Simply talk to the client. Depending on the client and circumstances, you might email, write a letter, or make a phone call. The message is plain and simple: "You must treat my employees in a civil manner."

In our case, this is a single warning situation. We assume the first offense is a fluke related to having a bad day – and very little self-control. On the second offense, we inform the client that they must treat our employees with respect or we will terminate the contract. There is simply no reason that our employees must put up with abuse from within our organization, or from our clients.

In twenty years we have warned three clients and fired one for this behavior.

I've heard of cases where companies put up with abusive clients for long periods of time. In my opinion, this is inexcusable. Many of us go into business because of abusive and arrogant bosses. We owe it to our employees to avoid creating this kind of environment.

The other two kinds of phone abuse are less clear and easy to see. They consist of abusing your rules and processes.

Very often, we think we need to make ourselves available at all times to our clients. This simply is not true. Eventually, we begin to set up limits, processes, and procedures.

But some clients honestly believe they are "above the rules" and that they can get better support by forcing themselves upon you. I'm not sure how people get to be this way, but you need to enforce your rules and keep them from disrupting your business.

First, you need an official flow chart of how telephone calls and service requests are handled. Regarding service requests, see the chapter in Volume Four of this set: “How Do Service Requests Get Into Your System?” I recommend that you have a very clear system for getting service requests into your PSA (ticketing) system and communicate this to your clients.

Second, you should set up your PSA system so that clients can enter their own tickets by web or email. In addition, you should have a telephone process for creating service requests. In this manner, clients can enter tickets by a number of methods.

All new service tickets should trigger a text message to your service manager or the coordinator of the day. In this way, the service department will be aware of the new ticket in the fastest possible time frame and be able to start working the service ticket as quickly as possible.

It is critically important that you can honestly say to your clients: "The fastest way to get service is to enter a ticket in the system."

Once you have such a system in place, then phone calls to individual technicians are not the fastest way to get service.

- Phone calls to the service manager are not the fastest way to get service
- Phone calls to the owner are not the fastest way to get service

- Phone calls to every cell phone in your company are not the fastest way to get service
- Phone calls to every extension in your company are not the fastest way to get service
- Ten phone calls with ten messages are not the fastest way to get service

In other words, simply abusing your processes and procedures will not get faster service. You need to be able to say this with complete honesty. In this way, Following your processes will always be the fastest way to get service.

Once you can say that, then you remind your clients that "urgency" is determined by the priority they set on the ticket (see the post Service Ticket Updates) and not by how many times they contact you by phone.

Implementation Notes

Putting this policy into action is pretty simple. First, you need those flow charts for phone calls and service tickets. Second, you need to educate your clients and your employees.

Third, you need to follow your own rules. That means you DON'T let clients interrupt you with the problem of the moment . . . even if you're between service requests. The system is designed so that you are always working from highest priority to lowest priority, and from oldest to newest ticket. Any time you violate this rule, you train your clients that they can call you whenever they want, that urgent phone calls get more attention than tickets entered into the system properly, and that breaking your processes is the way to get things done.

Benefits

In the long run, you have these processes for a reason. They're not just arbitrary things you do to piss people off.

If you believe that working from highest to lowest priority is important, and that you should not be interrupt-driven, then you need to create systems that make those things happen. Working from highest to lowest priority reduces the overall workload in your office, it reduces stress, and it keeps clients happy.

In our modern society, we all want everything right now. Everything's urgent. But when you tell people to stop and think, they realize that these policies are necessary so that you can stay profitable and stay in business. That serves them best in the long run.

Three Take-Aways from This Chapter:

1. Remember: You are NOT interrupt-driven. Manage the phone calls or they will manage you.
2. Never put up with abusive clients – on the phone or in person.
3. Develop processes so that the fastest way to get service is through the ticketing system – not the telephone.

Three Action Steps for Your Company:

1. ____

____

2. ____

____

3. ____

____

43

Removing a Client from Managed Services

Whether you like it or not, sometimes you need to remove clients. Of course there are many reasons for this: You fire them, they quit you, they go out of business, they are merged with another company, etc. If they are managed service clients, you've got some cleaning up to do.

This is a time to be particularly careful about **money**. One of the best policies you can put in place is that ALL work – 100% of everything – must be paid in advance once a client gives notice. After all, once the relationship is over, there's not as much motivation to pay in a timely manner. Collect a small block of prepaid labor and plan to rebate the unused portion when all the work is complete.

In Volume Three of this series we'll discuss setting up new clients and we provide a checklist. That's mostly a service-delivery discussion. Here we talk about removing a client, which involves both the front office and the tech department. So we have to reverse that process with a different checklist. Of course there are a few more steps to add.

A Few Notes

First, you should give the client a "What's Next" Memo so they understand your policies from their cancellation notice to the end of the contract. This memo should include the following:

- Note that all labor to remove the client from managed services is billable (as an add/move/change it would not be covered under managed service).
- Note that the machines may be left in an unsafe state. Unless there's a billable ticket to turn on updates of some type, the machines will not receive critical updates after you remove your RMM (remote monitoring and management) agent. If anti-virus is included in your service, the machines will be without anti-virus unless there's a billable ticket to install something.
- Note reminding the client that your contract forbids them from hiring your employees without compensating you.
- Note that your company has and will abide by a non-disclosure agreement with the client company.
- Note that you will assist the client's new tech support (internal or external) with the transition, and that all labor related to that will be billable.
- Note that you will be giving the client all documentation and a summary of all outstanding issues with their machines.

Second, if the client purchases other services from you, or receives services "bundled" with the monthly maintenance service, you need to determine whether any of these services will continue. For example, if you bundle spam filtering and anti-virus in your monthly offering, is the client going to continue buying these services from you?

Clarify with the client that other contracts will remain in place (e.g., BDR, HAAS, or telephone).

Basically, you want to be as friendly and accommodating as possible. And you want to make sure you keep the client as informed as possible. Leaving with class may serve you well down the road. Who knows, you might get this client back one day.

Here's a sample **Checklist for Removing a Client From Managed Services**. This checklist routes from the administrative department to the tech department and then back to admin.

There is a Word docx format version of this checklist in the downloadable content that accompanies this book.

Remove Client from Managed Services - Checklist

Client: __________

Date: __________

Date service will stop: __________

Who at client office is our primary contact during transition?

____

Contact Phone __________

Contact Email __________

If there's another consultant we need to work with, note here:

____

Contact Phone __________

Contact Email __________

Routing Step One - Admin Dept.

- Review client's account
    - If there are any accounts receivable, make arrangements for payment.
- Contact client to inform them that all work to remove them from service is billable and all labor must be paid in advance.
- Collect prepayment of $__________ for __________ hours labor.
- Cancel automated recurring billing at merchant service.
- Set expiration date for Managed Service Monthly Recurring billing contracts in PSA.
    - Leave Billable Time and Materials contract in place and active.
    - Leave other monthly contracts in place (BDR, telephones, etc.).
    - If client will continue with "un-bundled" services, create recurring billing for these.
- If necessary, change client "terms" in QuickBooks.
- Will client still receive our newsletter? (Yes)(No)
    - If no, remove them from the newsletter mailing list.

Routing Step Two - Tech Dept.

- Create a billable service request to remove client from managed service.
- Note: All work related to removing agents, services, etc. from managed services is billable and should be logged against this ticket.
- If removing email filtering:
    - Create a billable ticket to remove from spam filter service.
    - Determine where email should be pointed.
    - Update MX records and other DNS as needed
    - Test that email is flowing before you close this ticket.
- Create a client summary report of all existing issues and tickets.
    - Service manager will email this to client.
- Verify that all documentation is up to date.
    - Deliver a copy of client documentation to client in paper or electronic format.
    - Be sure that client has a narrative description of their backup system.
- Determine whether any open tickets need to be worked before service is discontinued. Service manager will determine whether each of these is covered by the contract that is ending or is billable.
- Close all open tickets for this client that will not be worked. Add a note to each that the ticket was closed without completing service due to end of contract.

When all tickets are closed . . .

- Remove Continuum (or other) RMM agents.
    - Note: unless there is a ticket to set up automatic updates or another service, we are ONLY removing our agents.
- Update the daily monitoring documentation so we don't report all those machines as missing.
- Update Managed Services Grid

Routing Step Three - Admin Dept.

- If the client will be 100% gone, set the expiration date for the Time and Materials contract in the PSA.

When all invoices are paid and everything is settled . . .

- File all paperwork related to this client.
- Remove paper contract(s) for this client from the "current contracts" folder and place in client folder.
- Add this completed checklist to client folder

end of checklist

Three Take-Aways from This Chapter:

1. Create a checklist to manage the removal of a client from services. Make it as complete as possible.
2. Manage the money first: Put policies in place so that you do not lose money when a client leaves.
3. This checklist will be passed between departments. Make sure it doesn't get lost!

Three Action Steps for Your Company:

1. ____

   ____

2. ____

   ____

3. ____

   ____

Appendix A: Definitions and Acronyms

A/P (AP) Accounts Payable.

A/R (AR) Accounts Receivable.

ACH Automated Clearing House – a system that enables you to make payments directly from your bank account.

BDR Backup and Disaster Recovery. Generally, this term is used to refer to a device – a BDR device.

CAP Certified Authorization Professional. More information at https://www.isc2.org.

Checklist The name given to the finest level of detail for executing the action steps needed to achieve a result. A procedure should include at least one checklist, but might include more than one checklist.

CISSP Certified Information Systems Security Professional. More information at https://www.isc2.org.

COGs Cost of Goods Sold

Cost of Goods Sold	What you pay for the things you sell. Used to align financial categories so you can determine profitability on each category.
CSSLP	Certified Secure Software Lifecycle Professional. More information at https://www.isc2.org.
D.B.A.	"Doing Business As" statement. Also called a Fictitious Business Name application.
DOA	Dead on Arrival. Equipment that does not work when you take possession of it.
HaaS	Hardware as a Service. Any scheme in while you supply hardware to client for a monthly recurring fee rather than selling them the hardware to them.
LOB	Line of Business application. A type of software specific to a given industry (or line of business).
Markup	The amount or percentage you add to COGs – cost of goods – to arrive at your sale price.
NDB	Network Documentation Binder
Process	The name given to a series of tasks that result in a general outcome. A process might include several different procedures.
Procedure	The name given to a specific set of action steps that achieve an outcome.
Profit	The portion of revenue that you get to keep, after you deduct expenses and the cost of goods sold.

Profit Margin	See profit. "Margin" refers to the portion of the sale that you get to keep. Profit is often describe in dollars while margin is often described as a percentage. They come from the same numbers.
PSA	Professional Services Administration. A type of software that includes modules for running your professional service business.
Revenue	Revenue is income: The total amount of money that you bring into the organization.
ROI	Return on Investment
SBS	Small Business Server
SMB	Small and Medium Business
SOP	Standard Operating Procedures
SPLA	Service Provider Licensing Agreement from Microsoft. This is a program in which you reselling Microsoft licensing for a low monthly fee and make monthly payments to Microsoft based on the total number of licenses deployed.
SSCP	Systems Security Certified Practitioner. More information at https://www.isc2.org.

Appendix B: Resources

Articles

The Cost of Interrupted Work: More Speed and Stress by Gloria Mark, Department of Informatics, University of California, Irvine and Daniela Gudith and Ulrich Klocke, Institute of Psychology, Humboldt University, Berlin, Germany. See http://www.ics.uci.edu/~gmark/chi08-mark.pdf

Is Money an Effective Motivator at Work? by Taras Bereza. www.word-mart.com/html/ is_money_an_effective_motivato.html

Worker, Interrupted: The Cost of Task Switching http://www.fastcompany.com/articles/2008/07/interview-gloria-mark.html

Workus Interruptus by Jeff Merron. http://www.slate.com/articles/news_and_politics/hey_wait_a_minute/2006/03/workus_interruptus.html

The Worst Sales Call *Ever* by Karl W. Palachuk. http://blog.smallbizthoughts.com/2008/10/worst-sales-call-ever.html

Books

Drive by Daniel Pink.

The E-Myth Revisited by Michael E. Gerber.

First Things First by Stephen R. Covey, A. Roger Merrill, and Rebecca R. Merrill.

Managed Services in a Month by Karl W. Palachuk.

The Network Migration Workbook by Karl W. Palachuk and Manuel L. Palachuk. www.networkmigrationworkbook.com.

The Power of Focus by Jack Canfield.

Project Management in Small Business by Dana Goulston, PMP, and Karl W. Palachuk.

Relax Focus Succeed by Karl W. Palachuk. www.relaxfocussucceed.com.

Service Agreements for SMB Consultants by Karl W. Palachuk. www.serviceagreementsforsmbconsultants.com.

Software and Services

99designs.com. www.99designs.com. A site where you can post a "contest" to have artists compete for your graphic design work.

ASCII Group. www.ascii.com. A membership-based group for technology companies. ASCII is both a buying group for services and a community for sharing ideas and best practices.

Autotask. www.autotask.com. One of the most successful PSA systems.

Business Plan Pro software. www.paloalto.com/business_plan_software

ConnectWise PSA. See www.connectwise.com. One of the most successful PSA systems.

Elance. www.elance.com. A site for finding outsourced talent from around the world.

Odesk. www.odesk.com. A site for finding outsourced talent from around the world.

The One Page Business Plan products www.onepagebusinessplan.com/books2.htm

Quosal. www.quosal.com.

QuoteWerks. www.quotewerks.com.

Misc. Web Sites

Internal Revenue Service (U.S.) – http://www.irs.gov

Also http://www.irs.gov/Businesses/Small-Businesses-&-Self-Employed/Starting-a-Business

And http://www.irs.gov/Businesses/Small-Businesses-&-Self-Employed/Recommended-Reading-for-Small-Businesses

ITSecurity.com – Source for security audit fodder. http://www.itsecurity.com/features/it-security-audit-010407/

Microsoft Partner Program – http://www.microsoft.com/partner

OvernightPrints.com – http://www.overnightprints.com – A good source for getting business cards printed.

Send Out Cards – https://www.sendoutcards.com.

SMBBooks.com – The primary book store for Karl's books. Also the place where you can register this book to access downloadable content.

Social Security information – http://www.ssa.gov/policy/docs/quickfacts/prog_highlights

uprinting.com – http://www.uprinting.com – A good source for getting business cards printed.

U.S. Small Business Administration – http://www.sba.gov/content/learn-about-your-state-and-local-tax-obligations

Vista Print – http://www.vistaprint.com – A good source for getting business cards printed.

Other Resources from Small Biz Thoughts

Please Check Out Our Web Sites:

www.SMBBooks.com

This is our primary site for books on technical topics, managed services, running your business, and more. All of our up-coming training events and recorded programs are there as well.

www.SmallBizThoughts.com

blog.SmallBizThoughts.com

This is our primary web site and Karl's popular blog for I.T. Consultants and Managed Service Providers. You can also find out about SOPs (standard operating procedures) and business coaching through this web site.

Karl's Weekly Newsletter

Register at one of the sites above or at GreatLittleBook.com.

This newsletter covers upcoming events, seminars, news, and "what's happening" in the SMB Consulting space.

Please also consider these fine books by Great Little Book:

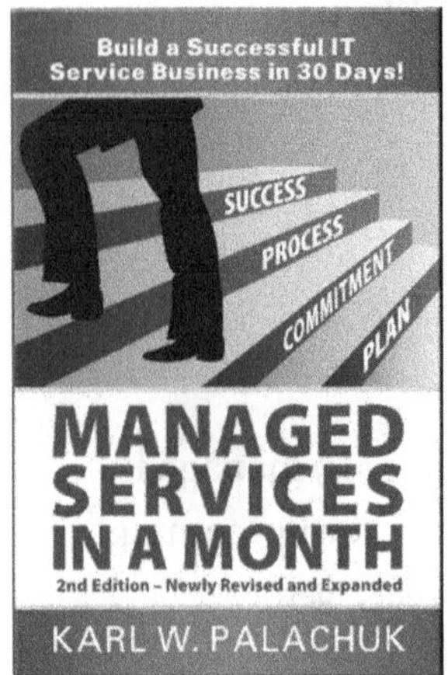

Managed Services in a Month 2nd ed.

Build a Successful IT Services Business in 30 Days.

by Karl W. Palachuk

2013

208 pages

A no-nonsense guide to building a successful managed service practice.

Whether you are just starting out, or converting your existing break/fix technology consulting business to managed services, this book will show you the way. The newly revised and expanded 2nd edition has nine new chapters, covering the latest products and services available today-including cloud technologies.

Also available as an e-book, audio book, or in a Spanish language translation.

The #1 book on Managed Services on Amazon.com for more than five years!

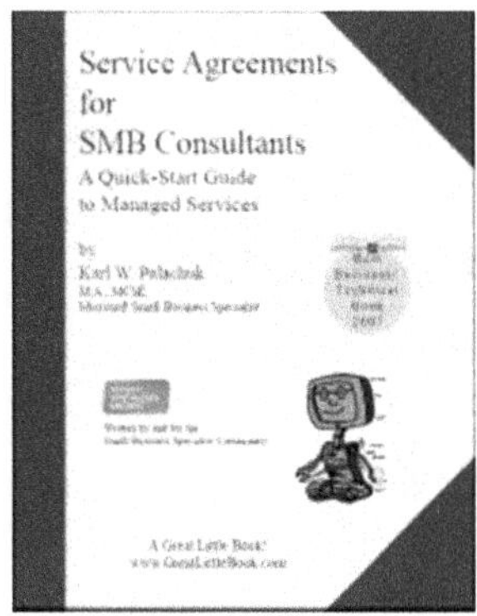

Service Agreements for SMB Consultants

A Quick-Start Guide to Managed Services

by Karl W. Palachuk

2006

185 pages

This great little book does a lot more than give you sample agreements.

Karl starts out with a discussion of how you run your business and the kinds of clients you want to have. The combination of these – defining yourself and defining your clients – is the basis for your service agreements.

Includes sample contracts with commentaries. All text, as well as some other great resources are provided as downloads.

Available in paperback or e-book formats.

www.SMBBooks.com

www.SmallBizThoughts.com

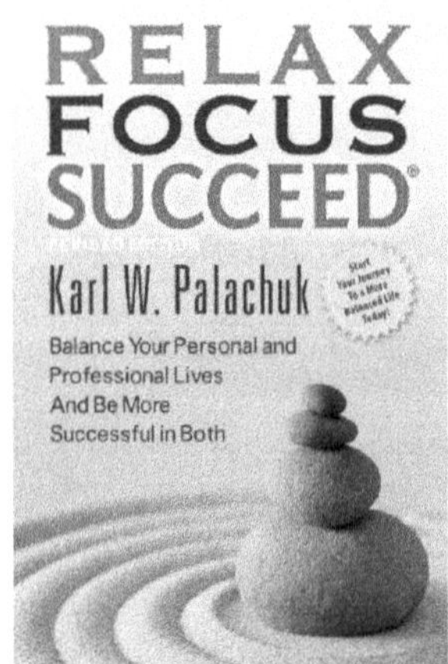

Relax Focus Succeed®

Balance Your Personal and Professional Lives and Be More Successful in Both

by Karl W. Palachuk

2013

296 pages

The premise of this book is simple but powerful: The fundamental keys to success are focus, hard work, and balance. Too often, the advice we receive gives plenty of attention to focus and hard work, but very little to balance.

This great little book will help you believe that you need balance, show you the power of focus, and help you move forward with the new you -- a happier, healthier, better balanced, and more successful you.

www.SMBBooks.com

www.SmallBizThoughts.com

www.ingramcontent.com/pod-product-compliance
Lightning Source LLC
Chambersburg PA
CBHW060807220326
41598CB00022B/2558

* 9 7 8 0 9 9 0 5 9 2 3 2 7 *